D1566608

"This exquisitely written book overflows with the kind of transformational wisdom, inspired storytelling and unexpected humor that leads to joyful communion with our higher self. For anyone looking to change their mind into a trusted ally in the search for enduring peace and happiness, *Mind What Matters* receives our highest recommendation."

Gerald G. Jampolsky, M.D. & Diane Cirincione-Jampolsky, Ph.D,
Founders of Attitudinal Healing International
&
Authors of *A Mini Course for Life*

Related Work by John Viscount

Admissions
A Film For Peace
Winner of 26 International Awards
Starring Academy Award® nominee James Cromwell
www.admissionsfilm.com

"This is an AMAZING FILM.
Easily my favorite film of the year."

Sharon Stone
Actress/Activist/Mother

MIND WHAT MATTERS

Mind What Matters

A Pep Talk for Humanity

John Viscount

Edited By
Teal Ferguson And Kenneth Kales

Cover Art By
Michael Goodnight, Kent Land And John Viscount

Inside Art By
Mike Murray And John Viscount

Deepest Gratitude to:

My father Robert, my mother Teal, and my brothers Bob, Tom and Mike for the abundant wisdom, creativity and gifts you bring to my life and the world.

Special Acknowledgements to:

Teal Ferguson, Elisabeth Feiss, Michael Smith, Gary Wintz, Wassana Sanlar, Wendy Newman, Craig Janik, Kent Land, Tim Agee, Michael Goodnight, Gavin Behrman, Donald Cassel, Gavin Graves, Marc Van Marter and the Mind Over Fabric crew - Merlan Land, Jade Lee, Greg Mathis, Saveida Vasquez, Mike Murray, Matt Smith, Heather Staley, Sylvia Castillo, Jose Aguinaga, Friedia Niiumra, Sara Ohara and Shaina Fast for your selfless support that made this book possible.

Profound Thanks to:

George Sengstack and the Sengstack family - Dr. George Sengstack, Cinda, Mary, Jane and Howard, Michael, Lisa and Alexandra Pompa and the Pompa family, Ramiro Medina and the Medina family, Mac Squier and the Squier family, Julie Taylor and the Taylor family, Sally Viscount and the Crawford family, Ken Hirsch, Matt Yelton, Tracy, Brian, Nick and Taylor Viscount, Terry, Katy and Maddy Tierney, Jordan Snow, Ryan Cinelli, Harry Kakatsakis, Antonia Sweeney, Lisa, Aurora, Lynn, Arnold and Matt Behrman, Rex Openshaw, Andrew and Stephanie Pelmoter and the Pelmoter family, the *Admissions* family, Chuck Minsky, Wes Shrum, Rick Duque, Rono and Sierra Smith, Roy and Melba Slavin, Ehrin Van Marter, Jennifer, Brighton, Zyan and Danner Graves, Jennifer Banovetz, Richard Parkinson, Libby and Len Traubman, Todd Levine, Linda Harris, Joe Fletcher, Steven Santoro,

James Cromwell, Oren Dayan, Anna Khaja, Anthony Batarse, Harry Yoon, Walter and Nettie Propps, Joe Phelps and the Phelps Group family, Glenn Schieke, Catharina Go, Gerald G. Jampolsky, Diane Cirincione-Jampolsky, Saul Arbess, Mike Abkin, Anne Creter and The Global Alliance for Ministries & Infrastructures for

Peace, Scott Bruer, Lisa Elias and the PeaceNow family, Aajonus Vonderplanitz, Peter Joseph, Sharleen Bazeghi, Nico, Stosh, Ray and Sam Janik, Uri Lee and Troy Casey, Larry Nisonoff, Doug Davies, Lance Van Winter, Wayne Blake, Mark Basile, Chrissy Pray, Stan Preston, Karen Allen, Kate Nelligan, Jared Rosen, Bill Gladstone, Kenneth Kales, John Raatz, Beverly Hutchinson, Steve Robertson, Shirley Van Marter, Brendan Kenny, Grace Fritzinger, Don Weir and Sara Daly Weir, Rod McBrian, Dorothy Picciano, Jere Daly, Brent Whitaker, Jeff Kelly and the Kelly family, Jeff Pompa, Mike Long, Kyle and Nada Ryan, Rob Hamilton, Paul Canterna, Steve Mackall, Rebel Steiner, Katie Ramsay, Sandy Hochman, David Carlson, Chris Greenleaf, Joey Daddario, Ted Sprague, Francis Sullivan, Jim Agee, Craig Eastman, Michael Walters, Matt Garagusi, Jim Herman, Frank Jannotta, Stewart Cooley, Bob Nelson, Jason Rath, Mike Lapchick, Kevin Douglas, Analani Patterson, Dave Silver, Marc Bruno, Paul Garver, John Bouman, Charley Hatch, Steve Crow, Rick Salamanca (and all the rest of my brothers' great friends), Jon Blitz and the Fernwood, Pyle, Silver Bullet and Walt Whitman soccer families, Courtland Ferguson and the Ferguson family, Katherine Viscount and the Viscount family, Zain Effendi, Saul Glazer, Dave Herman, John Hayes, Melanie Murray, Anne Elizabeth Grace, Pat and Rama Jager, Eric Simon, Chip, Susan, Kalie and Nika Feiss and the Elisabeth Feiss community, Molly McGinn, Susan Adams, Jack Wintz, Tese Neighbor, Fandra Chang, Vanessa Schreiber, Michelle Berc, Rebecca Crandel, Carol Kelly, Susan Woodfield, Mary Cook, Cammy Banks, Jaime Hillis, Pimpilai Shrawder, Randy Beer, Junior, May Hattan, Max, Michael Tansill, Allison Porter, Melissa Perez, Paul Van Wart, Hughes Kraft, Doug Meyer, Michael Nemrow, Randy Widder, Stan Preston, General Balmer, Vaughn Verdi, Peter Sprague, Neil Gates, Samantha Simms, Jin Natale, Christian Bonello, Ren Blanco, Allison and Ian Band, Mike Cassel, Mark Squier, Jeff Nelson, Paul Wenhold, Adam Holiber, Stan Hough, John Hough, Joel Greenzaid, Lew Blakey, John Keating, Lou Caceres, Eric Beringer, Tom Miller, Richard Moskovitz, Lynn McGrew, Linda Breggin, Burt Harrell,

Jennifer Charlton, Dr. William O'Meara, Bill Steiniger, Ramona Pavis, Ed and Carole Kim, Stephanie Thai, Jaymee Del Rosario, Joann Henderson, John Kelly, Mitch, Alexa and Joely Newman, Pat Reed and Teal's tennis family, John and Lorena Devlin, Dave Jones, James Cooley, Mistik, Loomer, Wylie, Pheenix, Micky, Brooke, Sylvie, Lisa, Lara, Art, Mark, Tom, Cassandra, Derek, Ariane, Floater, Aaron, Travis, Mack, Nibbler and all the great folks my memory does not serve...for the love, inspiration, music, laughter, friendship and great conversations that opened my heart and expanded my mind.

CONTENTS

INTRODUCTION

The best day of my life was the day I realized I was insane. That was when it finally dawned on me that I couldn't trust my mind to think the right thing or to see the world in a way that would bring me peace.

It was at that moment that I realized it was up to me, and only me, to train my mind to be an asset, rather than a hindrance. Otherwise it was going to continue to make my life extremely difficult.

Up to that point, I had no idea that it was my thinking that was flawed because I couldn't use my own closed mind as a tool to see more clearly. Somehow I had to wake up and break free of my own mind. The alternative was I would be imprisoned for life by my lack of self-awareness and mental control.

As the frustration mounted and then manifested in unhealthy ways through cluster headaches, ulcers, relationship struggles and an overall lack of peace, I finally came to the realization that there had to be a better way.

So I began searching, mainly through the teachings of great wisdom teachers. I entered an intense and rewarding period of self-education that has not diminished over the years. The more I studied and opened up my mind, the more I realized that a lot of people had wise things to teach me.

From spiritual teachers to philosophers, from statesmen to scientists, from soldiers to poets, from psychologists to business people, from artists to writers to the everyday person on the street, they all contributed to the wealth of great thinking the human mind has gifted the world.

I dedicated my life to learning what they had learned and adopting whatever helped me the most. I benefited from this practice so much that I eventually wanted to share some of the wisdom I had experienced. This led me to launch a line of clothing that features positive messages inspired by transformational teachings. At the time, I wrote this essay to explain my reasons for creating the line and even more importantly to illuminate the rewarding nature of the inward path.

The Endless Joy of the Spiritual Mutt

Life is complicated.

We wake up to sudden consciousness, as a tenderhearted baby on a big, blue planet that's been swallowed whole by an endless universe. The only thing more perplexing than our birth is what we're supposed to do with ourselves afterwards.

When we finally settle on a plan, we discover we can't possibly know where we're headed because where we're headed changes the second we arrive. To gain some control over our affairs, we spend much of our time reliving the past or safeguarding the future, neither of which is actually possible. We find it most difficult to live in the present moment, even though it is the only moment in which we can actually live.

Fortunately, one of the many advantages of living nowadays is all the wise and compassionate souls who have already been here and done this and have been kind enough to leave directions. When blended into the hybrid worldview of a spiritual mutt, these wonderfully mixed and varied breeds of wisdom can serve as loyal guides on the path to happiness.

This is especially true in today's complex world where we are taught to spend decades mastering advanced skills with which to pursue careers, wealth and respect to theoretically achieve fulfillment. But often we aren't able to devote even a few seconds a day to mastering our own heart and creating a mood within it that will make every single endeavor, from doing the dishes to simply breathing, peaceful and rewarding.

I became a spiritual mutt because, more often than not, I was like an unhappy Greyhound speeding in circles around life's racetrack chasing the illusory rabbit just beyond my reach. I kept looking on the outside for something that was right there on the inside all along.

One day some friends and I stumbled upon some powerfully positive teachings and began diving into the riches of wisdom in bookstores and libraries. We found that just a few words of wisdom could help us achieve some real happiness by simply reminding us to enjoy this instant . . . this instant.

Inspired by the truths we were experiencing, I began distilling them down into positive messages and started looking for a way to share them. The idea of clothing seemed like a good fit because even though most people aren't able to spend much time dressing their hearts each day, I knew they still had to dress their bodies.

In the end, it seemed like it was worth a try because an increase in even one person's happiness would be an increase in happiness for the whole world.

So you might say Mind Over Fabric is the expression of the unconditional love and endless joy of the spiritual mutt, greeting you with wagging tail at the doors of your awareness, playfully inviting you in to the abundant peace and beauty of the human heart.

I hope our messages bring some great energy your way.

This book is the next stage in that journey.

By sharing a few of the lessons I have learned from my own struggles and mistakes and the spiritual quest for which they were a catalyst, I hope to offer others a little easier ride through life. I guess you can kind of think of me as your personal crash test dummy.

In these writings, certain core themes are occasionally repeated – forgiveness, oneness, unity, right mind, wrong mind, separation, shared interests – because learning of this kind is only achieved through repetition. The mind can be amazingly stubborn and resistant to change. That's why transformation is usually only attained through "spiritual practice."

With any luck, I am hoping you will find something helpful in these pages that nourishes your thinking the way it did mine, and you will grow to realize as I did that, in the end, a kind, loving and forgiving mind is what matters most.

Peace,

John Viscount

1
LIFE IS WORTH THE TRIP

I recently stopped by to visit an old friend who had been placed in an Alzheimer's ward. When I entered the cheerfully decorated facility, a sunny receptionist told me the code to punch into the security doors to get back to the rooms. Considering the world to which it was gaining me access, it kind of felt like a code to nowhere. It was the same code that they had told me numerous times on previous visits but, for the life of me, I could never seem to remember it. This sometimes made me wonder if I was visiting my future home.

As I made my way down the long hallway that was powerfully scented with disinfectants, I passed by a large group of Alzheimer's patients. They were all in various stages of the disease's woeful journey and with each one I walked by, I felt myself questioning why this world exists. I wondered who drew it up and how so much suffering slipped into the final product line.

But hey, who am I to try to address the mysteries of the origin of the universe, right? Well, actually, a member of the human race, that's who, one of the universe's most deeply tormented tenants, the one with tons of big questions and very few big answers. Maybe you're familiar with the type?

But back to "Old Timer's" disease, which is what I thought it was called when I first heard of it. It almost sounded quaint until I visited my friend at her final home on Earth and got served reality.

Walking through an Alzheimer's ward is like visiting a recreation center filled with nice, normal, everyday folks who have not been told they have been given LSD. On the outside, they still appear to be living in the world and in their body. But in actuality, they are somewhere else entirely, located solely in the feverish dreams inside their heads. Judging by their deep immersion in what only they can see, it becomes instantly obvious they are completely unaware their projections aren't reality. Or at least their projections aren't *my reality*. I have my own projections for that.

Some, the lucky ones perhaps, just stare ahead blankly like abandoned homes with just a single, one-watt light bulb left on. Others, the more lively ones, included me seamlessly into their random conversations as if I had been there talking all along. Each came off as a *maitre d'* of the absurd, dishing up one hallucination after the other with the smooth authority of a Beverly Hills restaurant host ticking off the night's specials.

One cute, nattily dressed, blue-haired lady pulled me aside and told me with convincing earnestness to make sure I put away the nonexistent peanut butter she held in her right hand after I was finished spreading it on the nonexistent bread she held in her left hand.

A kindly, gray-haired gentleman happily greeted me like his long-lost son, picking up right where our father-son relationship had left off in his addled mind. For a little while I even played along. I thought, how could it hurt? At least for that brief moment we both felt loved.

A hunched-over grandmotherly type alternated between laughing hysterically and cursing to high heaven. All middle roads seemed to have been erased from her mind and she was now living at the mercy of her imagined extremes. I found her easy to relate to.

A middle-aged gentleman repeatedly looked under his seat as if searching for the trap door leading out of the patchy nowhere world into which he had somehow fallen.

On top of all the well-meaning hallucinators seemingly around every corner, another reason a walk through an Alzheimer's ward feels so surreal is that no one is really connecting with anyone else. It's just a series of human islands floating in space with no bridges to link them. When I finally got to my friend's door I actually had to take a moment to remember who I was because the compelling performances I had just witnessed had loosened my own sense of self.

My friend was alone in her little room, on her little bed, with her face, arms and hands rigidly clenched as if someone had sprayed her with quick-drying invisible cement during the peak of an all-world temper tantrum. Her claw-like hands extended upward, beyond her covers, reaching for something important, but never finding it. Her expression was that of a soul-piercing, silent scream.

In her excruciating pose, I could almost see the suffering of all humanity scratched out in the deep furrows on her forehead and around her eyes. Each worn-in groove told its own tale, and then told it over and over again, the tread marks of well-traveled adversity.

My friend would remain frozen in silent, pantomimed agony for 15 minutes at a time until, from deep down, an unnerving scream would climb out of the bowels of her being and pierce the ward's sleep-inducing Muzak. It got me thinking.

Where is the hope in this?

My friend started out as a fresh, young human being, fearless and energized, ready to take on the world and begin an epic adventure. She grew up in Venice, California, fell in love, got married and had a strong career in broadcast television. She had loving friends and pets, traveled the world, joined spiritual groups, walked the beach under the moonlight and even gained faith in God.

And then this.

But as I sat by her bedside and watched her play a role she didn't consciously sign up for and struggled to find peace with her rapidly deteriorating condition, suddenly an unexpected thing happened. What had seemed so pointless became profound. What had seemed so depressing now began to lift me up. How? I had found hope.

The hope that the chance to experience life and share the wonderful love we have with family, friends and loved ones is worth going through anything for, even a stay at an Alzheimer's ward on your way out of Dodge. The hope that it is our mind that has the final say on what our life experience will be and this will always give us the ability to find the motivation to go on.

No doubt, what our eyes see in this world at times can seem hopeless. But thankfully, our minds don't have to concur. We don't have to see the "reality" we think we see in front of our face as the ultimate reality. And in this loophole there is endless hope because it allows us to make our mind an agent of inspiration instead of despair.

So instead of focusing on the deep sadness I felt seeing fellow human beings struggling with Alzheimer's, I saw hope in the low-paid, dedicated staff tending to their brothers and sisters in need.

I saw hope in the loving visits from friends and family, even when there was no recognition in their loved one's eyes.

I saw hope in the social events that had been meticulously planned for the residents, even though most won't be "present" for them.

I saw hope that, even with the bleakest afflictions, humans have created loving ways to take care of each other.

I saw hope that the methods we use to care for each other are always improving, and this means the level of compassion in the world is rising.

Finally, I saw hope in how my friend held my hand and wouldn't let go and how that made us connected, even in a supremely disconnected place like an Alzheimer's ward. In fact, there is hope all around; you just have to learn how to see it.

Today, use the powerful tool that is your mind to uncover hope where you have never seen it before. Show the world how hope can change perceptions and, when it does, it changes lives for the better. Show the world that the experience of having hope is in many ways just as rewarding as anything you could possibly hope for. Show the world what positive visionaries and their hopeful brethren have always known, when hope is your traveling companion, life is worth the trip.

VOICES

Hope is like the sun, which, as we journey toward it, casts the shadow of our burden behind us.

Samuel Smiles

You will face many defeats in your life, but never let yourself be defeated.
Maya Angelou

Hope sees the invisible, feels the intangible, and achieves the impossible.
Author Unknown

The pessimist sees difficulty in every opportunity. The optimist sees the opportunity in every difficulty.

Winston Churchill

Those who wish to sing always find a song.

Proverb

2

THE GREATEST POWER IN THE WORLD IS THE POWER TO CHOOSE YOUR REACTION TO THE WORLD

In life, nothing matters.
That is, unless you let it.

This simple fact means you possess the greatest power in the world, the power to create your actual life experience. No matter what happens to you, the experience of it comes down to you because you get to decide how you are going to respond to it. You have the absolute final say in all matters.

That's why real power is not demonstrated by conquering the world. Real power is exercised when we don't let the world conquer our mind. False power, on the other hand, is when we stop depending on our own mind for our peace and instead dive in to the ever-changing, external world in search of happiness.

By depending on external things to determine our mood, we are forced into making impossible demands such as that rain never falls within 50 miles of a wedding, that the stock market only goes up and unemployment only goes down, that freeways will empty every time we enter them, that every person we develop feelings for will develop similar feelings for us, that dictators will suddenly "enlighten up" and start sharing power, that our wrinkles will fall out and our hair will fall in, that our family, friends and loved ones will all outlive us, even though we hope to live forever. Welcome to your "wrong mind," the beginning of suffering and the end of peace.

Your "right mind," on the other hand, simply acknowledges that the external world is irrelevant to inner peace. Your right mind knows that in the external world only impermanence is permanent so there is no need to get too hung up on anything that happens there. Of course, this doesn't mean you should avoid the world. On the contrary, while you are passing through you should enjoy life's incredible bounty and learn as much as you can while you're here. This is putting the world to its best use.

But, on a deeper level, where it makes sense, surrender it. You are so much more than the world anyway. The way to prove it is by releasing it. This is right-minded thinking that addresses the only real problem in the world, our extreme attachment to it. Once we fix that, all other problems tend to cease to matter.

If you think this is an impossible thing to accomplish and are in need of some real life inspiration, just consider the intrepid band members on the Titanic. Legend has it that these wise, undaunted souls kept playing their music as the great ship sank into the frigid waters. By making the choice to play on they made sure it was their reaction to life that became their life experience, rather than the conditions of their life.

Their famous final encore has to go down as one of the most powerful performances in history, and I am not talking about their music. In essence, they played the world rather than let the world play them. And, as their music filled the air for all to hear they regained ultimate power over their lives.

Or look at the example that Mahatma Gandhi set. By following the doctrine of non-violence, he chose his reaction to the unfair and often violent system of rule the British Empire had imposed on India. By rising above the battleground, he made the most eloquent argument possible for the inherent worth of all Indians and, by extension, all human beings including the British.

He essentially aligned himself with an ideal rather than the circumstance he was presented with. When he did this, he made an elegant case for civil rights in his country and set an example for future leaders across the globe. In the process, he ushered in a better, more equitable way for India and England to co-exist.

Or consider the life of Viktor Frankl, who wrote *Man's Search for Meaning*. Even in the human degradation and hopelessness of a German death camp in World War II, Frankl was able to exercise the most important freedom of all, the freedom to determine one's own attitude and inner well-being. The power of that choice still resonates today in everyone who reads his profoundly moving book. Below are his enlightened words describing his purpose in writing it:

"I had wanted simply to convey to the reader by way of concrete example that life holds a potential meaning under any conditions, even the most miserable ones. And I thought that if the point were demonstrated in a situation as extreme as that in a concentration camp, my book might gain a hearing. I therefore felt responsible for writing down what I had gone through, for I thought it might be helpful to people who are prone to despair."

Later in the book, he describes the power we all posses to choose our reaction to the world:

"We who lived in the concentration camps can remember the men who walked through the huts comforting others, giving away their last piece of bread. They may have been few in number, but they offer sufficient proof that everything can be taken away from a man but one thing: the last of the human freedoms – to choose one's attitude in any given set of circumstances, to choose one's own way.

"And there were always choices to make. Every day, every hour, offered the opportunity to make a decision, a decision which determined whether you would or would not submit to those powers that threatened to rob you of your very self, your inner freedom; which determined whether or not you would become the plaything of circumstance, renouncing freedom and dignity to become molded into the form of the typical inmate."

Dr. Frankl was able to take one of the bleakest experiences human beings have ever had to endure and exercise his inner freedom to determine what he would take away from it. And what was

Dr. Frankl's ultimate conclusion after his experience in concentration camps? Love is our highest calling.

After the war he became a leading psychiatrist and neurologist and founded Logotherapy, which is considered "The Third Viennese School of Psychotherapy" after Freud's psychoanalysis and Adler's individual psychology. According to Wikipedia, Logotherapy is based on three principles:

- Life has meaning under all circumstances, even the most miserable ones.
- Our main motivation for living is our will to find meaning in life.
- We have freedom to find meaning in what we do, and what we experience, or at least in the stand we take when faced with a situation of unchangeable suffering.

Not only was he not broken by the concentration camps, Dr. Frankl ended up taking his experiences and developing a new way to treat patients suffering from depression and mental illness. How is that for turning water into wine?

Today, experience some true liberty and free yourself from the bondage to the external world. You have everything you need to be happy right now, the power to choose your reaction to the world. It is the greatest power you possess and the one power the world can never take away from you. All you have to do is make up your mind.

Voices

Better indeed is knowledge than mechanical practice. Better than knowledge is meditation. But better still is surrender of attachment to results because there follows immediate peace.

Bhagavad Gita

Analysis does not set out to make pathological reactions impossible, but to give the patient's ego freedom to decide one way or another.

Sigmund Freud

Most of your reactions are echoes of the past. You do not really live in the present.

Gaelic Proverb

Each of us literally chooses, by his way of attending to things, what sort of universe he shall appear to himself to inhabit.

William James

Participate joyfully in the sorrows of the world. We cannot cure the world of sorrows, but we can choose to live in joy.

Joseph Campbell

3

HEART IS MIND'S
GREATEST TEACHER

Three cheers for the heart!!!
Can you imagine what life would be like without it? What would it feel like to not be able to feel? What would it feel like to not be able to cheer?

How would you really know what to do or the right choices to make? How would you really know what you were going through at any point in time? You would be lost in an endless emptiness, with no bearings and no real motivation to find your way out. There would be no point to existence.

Indeed, the mind separated from the heart is like sunlight without warmth, a marching band without a rhythm section, a love poem without passion, a compass without poles. The sometimes aching, sometimes breaking, sometimes soaring heart, is the core of life, the center of our emotional being, and without its energy and guidance life itself would become featureless.

This world is a complicated place in which we are called upon to make many decisions that will deeply impact our time on Earth and often determine its very essence. Throughout history, wisdom teachers have focused on the ability of the heart to guide us to truth and meaning and to help us avoid taking wrong turns into negative *cul-de-sacs*. The heart, it is often said, is our best set of eyes and is the place where true vision comes from. Therefore, it is the heart we should ask before every stage in our journey: Am I acting out of love or reacting out of fear?

If we are acting out of love then we can genuinely surrender all outcomes, sit back and enjoy the show. We have done our part to listen to our heart and follow our higher mind to higher ground. This choice is all that is required to experience an immediate increase in our PQ, our peace quotient. Acting out of love creates a quiet and effective mind, a certainty of purpose and a sense of worth and beauty. It provides joy with which to greet the day.

Even when life's more serious challenges come up, it is the heart that will show us the way. As circumstances appear to grow more dire, the heart's power of illumination only gets stronger. You can count on it to shine the brightest, in fact, when things are the darkest.

Mother Theresa, Martin Luther King and Jesus all utilized this kind of vision to see beyond the heartless thinking that led to some of history's most unfortunate detours into fear. To find the proper healing response to institutionalized class differences, racism and religious persecution, they consulted their hearts and looked at things with the eyes of love. When they did, it was clear that the greatest good for all was the only good that meant anything at all.

Each in their own way used their time living in a body to demonstrate that bodily differences mean nothing and the love that unites us is all that matters. They lived as if separation was ultimately illusory and proved that in joining together, we could heal what ails us. Because they acted out of love, their wisdom proved transformational to the world and remains so to this day.

By making a similar choice at every step in our own journey, we will ensure that the timeless, heart-directed thinking of great healers like these lives on. When our minds become distracted by things that don't matter and we become unsure about which path to take, we can look to the heart and the loving way forward will become clear.

Are you acting out of love or are you reacting out of fear? Ask yourself this as much as you can and it will become your guidance system on your journey to inner peace. Only your heart knows the answer for sure, so listen to it and take its counsel. If kindness becomes your way, kindness will become your life because giving and receiving are one and the same.

The energy we put out into the world creates the world we live in, and to this there is no exception. When we come from the heart and look for the good in everyone, we get to live in a world filled with folks we love. We will discover that we don't even have to know people personally to love them intensely. It might be a compelling picture on the internet or a story in the news or a stranger passing on the street. Come from the heart and we will feel compassion for all. A deeper connection to life will be our just reward.

On the other hand, when we stray from the heart and react out of fear, which happens to us all, we end up living in a world filled with things we fear. That's why in the final analysis the greatest reward or punishment in life is just being what we are. When we act out of love, love is what we become.

Today, cast the most important vote you can make in this world and elect your heart to be your mind's greatest teacher. Start to experience the sweet revelations its warm guidance will bring. Your life will become the most rewarding class you have ever taken.

VOICES

Educating the mind without educating the heart is no education at all.

Aristotle

The human heart feels things the eyes cannot see and knows what the mind cannot understand.

Robert Valet

There is a magnet in your heart that will attract true friends. That magnet is unselfishness, thinking of others first; when you learn to live for others, they will live for you.

Paramahansa Yogananda

I would rather have eyes that cannot see, ears that cannot hear, lips that cannot speak than a heart that cannot love.

Robert Tizon

A man of knowledge chooses a path with a heart and follows it and then he looks and rejoices and laughs and then he sees and knows.

Carlos Castaneda

Wherever you go, go with all your heart.

Confucius

4

CANCER IS A
MOTIVATIONAL SPEAKER

A s I write this, a very close, dear friend of mine, Elisabeth Feiss, is doing what most of the world would classify as "fighting cancer." It is a very aggressive form of cancer that keeps popping up in unexpected places, much to my friend's amazement and dismay. Through it all though Elisabeth has remained remarkably brave and full of grace. I have actually seen her in her hospital bed between grueling, successive operations taking calls from friends and asking them about *their* lives and counseling them about *their* problems. I have seen her travel the world for alternative treatments while compromising her financial security in the process, and yet not once heard her rail at the unfairness of it all. Does she get down? Of course. But she has held up remarkably well considering everything. I find her to be a wise teacher and feel lucky to know her.

Having spent a good deal of time with Elisabeth in the cancer environment, it has become clear that most folks see the condition as a titanic struggle, and as something to be terrified of and be on edge about 24/7. This is completely understandable considering the high stakes of the disease and the widespread apprehension of death in our world. Unfortunately though, holding cancer in this context is the worse thing we can do for our health. Because as it turns out, inner peace doesn't just make great spiritual sense, it makes great physical sense too.

Kinesiology tests have long confirmed what most of us have always felt, that fear makes the body go weak. So one way or the other, we must teach our selves to see cancer, whether we have it or not, in a non-fearful context. In fact, if cancer had a conscious brain, seeing us master our fear of it would be one of the things it would fear most. The courageous act of doing this not only deprives cancer of fuel. It also improves our quality of life and level of happiness, two other developments that make it harder for cancer to survive.

During World War II in an address to the nation, President Franklin Roosevelt wisely stated that we had "nothing to fear but fear itself." This wisdom applies just as much during times of peace and, even more so, when we are trying to overcome an illness like cancer. By dreading and fearing cancer, we give it unnecessary power over us and essentially play right into it.

If cancer were a boxer, it would be forever goading us to meet in the center of the ring to exchange blows because this makes it real and gives it strength. But in the history of boxing, no fighter has ever been better off physically for entering the ring. Of course we will still want to do whatever we feel we need to do on the physical level to cure cancer. But we will be much more effective with our physical efforts when our mind stays above the battleground.

As Buddhism teaches us, the key to mastering this world and our life is by staying out of the ring and remaining an observer. In other words, we don't master this world by mastering this world. We master this world by getting beyond this world, even while we are still living in it. We do this through learning detachment. And what is one of the best teachers of this all-important skill? Cancer, that ubiquitous motivational speaker now appearing at millions of venues across the globe.

In our impermanent earthly existence, the deep peace and mental well-being that are so critical to our physical health are never derived from being attached to the body. If you are expecting to permanently get all of your ducks in a row health-wise and to never have life-threatening conditions, it's better to surrender that thought right now. This realm is about learning, not permanence. As they say, life itself is a terminal illness, though I think it is much more fun to think of it as a terminal joy.

And who says this is a bad thing? We have no proof that the ephemeral quality of life is something to mourn. No one has ever come back from the hereafter and said, "Your income taxes will triple, your rent will quadruple, your body hair, finger nails and toe nails will grow a foot an hour, you'll commute to work on a donkey and every meal will be deep-fried spam."

On the contrary, souls that depart this realm are usually too busy diving into the next leg of their journey to hang around here, unless they become one of the many alleged ghosts in our world. And have you ever noticed how these misguided spirits are invariably of bad cheer? Yes, even our spectral friends have something to teach us about the dangers of becoming too attached to this world. That is, with the exception of Casper, that rare, well-adjusted, friendly ghost, which is only a cartoon after all.

Most souls move on, as they should. They have better things to do than hang around the old, stale haunts of their previous life. And thank goodness! Otherwise, we would exist in a perpetual stalemate. Mortality, for all the bad press it gets, keeps things moving. The best part about a great amusement park ride is that it comes to an end. After all, who wants to ride the same roller coaster forever? You would need a lot of barf bags. It is far more enjoyable to move on to the next ride with excitement in your heart and the wisdom you have gained to aid in your journey.

But back to our motivational speaker, cancer. How can we learn to see it as something other than totally frightening when it is trying to eat us from the inside out? Suddenly spiritual teachings seem out of their pay grade when our end is near and, to get there, we may have to travel through a lot of physical suffering.

We turn cancer into a teacher because this immediately gives us back some control and ensures the illness will be of some help to us, rather than something that just hurts us. We do this by utilizing cancer as an invaluable source of education. By getting beyond our immobilizing terror, we turn the tables and open our mind to the valuable lessons cancer has in store for us. In the best-case scenario, we let it establish some new, life-enhancing goals for ourselves.

For instance, what can cancer teach us about our lifestyle? Can it motivate us to take more vitamins, eat more raw, unprocessed food and take more nurturing walks in nature? Can it move us to meditate more and to give ourselves breaks from the endless pounding of our constant thinking? Can it compel us to read labels at the grocery store and to shop in the organic aisle?

What can it teach us about our level of appreciation? If we feel our time on Earth might be coming to an end, can this galvanize us to make the most of every moment, be better listeners and be more mindful in general? To reconnect with those who are important to us? To repair broken relationships, release grievances and come to peace with our selves and others?

Can it show us how to thoroughly enjoy a sunny day, a spring rain, a great book, an enlightening conversation, a healing nap, an expression of love, a deep breath or a beautiful coastline? Can it urge us to dive deeper into spiritual and religious teachings and to develop a faith in something bigger than our selves that can carry us through life with a steadying hand? Can it inspire us to put our time on Earth to better use and to dedicate it to the greater good? Can it ultimately be the catalyst that helps us prove that anything can be turned into a gift when we have a disciplined mind to assist us?

You bet it can and anything that can do all these things certainly has a lot of positives to offer us. Especially considering that these things need to be done regardless if we have cancer or not. And the sad truth is that it often takes a potentially terminal illness to get us to do these things.

When we feel we have plenty of time left we often leave the most important aspects of our life on the To Do list. But, by transforming cancer into a motivational speaker, now the thought of it can strengthen us and be the impetus for a more rewarding, self-actualized life rather than something that just weakens us. While it is motivating us in this fashion, we can also use cancer to teach us the most valuable skills in all of life, surrender and acceptance.

In 1969, Dr. Elisabeth Kubler Ross wrote a seminal book entitled, *On Death and Dying*. After conducting research and interviews with more than 500 dying patients, she put forth, *The Model of Coping with Dying*. In it, she describes in five distinct stages a process by which the people in her study coped with grief and tragedy, especially when diagnosed with a terminal illness.

The first stage is "denial," when people will say or think things like, "I feel fine, this can't be happening to me." This is usually a temporary stage that is eventually replaced by the realization of what will be left behind. This leads to the next stage of "anger," when people say or think things like, "How can this happen to me? It is not fair. Who or what is to blame?" This can be accompanied by feelings of rage and envy. The next stage is "bargaining," where the patient tries to negotiate with God or a higher power to delay or postpone death, often using the promise of a reformed lifestyle as a bargaining chip.

Next comes "depression," when the person starts to understand the certainty of death and may spend a lot of time grieving and crying. This begins the critical process of detaching from all the things the person loves and cherishes about life. The final stage is "acceptance," where they think things like, "It's probably going to be okay so I might as well prepare for it." This often leads to a deep, enduring peace previously not experienced in their lifetime. These stages not only deal with terminal illness, but also can occur in other life-altering events such as divorce or the end of a relationship or the loss of a job.

What stands out about her study is that only at detachment from the world does the patient experience any lasting peace. Based on this, it seems obvious that if we want a peaceful life then we need to start to learn detachment as early as we can, preferably about the same time we learn the alphabet. Ideally, this will enable us to shorten our time in the unpleasant first four stages in Dr. Kubler Ross's model and jump straight to detachment, acceptance and peace, not only as they relate to cancer, but to all aspects of life.

These skills are what keep us out of the boxing ring in our head where we typically fight against cancer and all the other things that befall us and inevitably end up in worse physical shape because of it. By staying in the bleachers and remaining a detached, silent witness, we give the things that happen to us much less ability to become us, even if they are literally consuming our bodies. Yes, this mental maneuver is hard to master and requires considerable discipline. But it is far from impossible. After all, we have the most powerful ally in the world. Our mind is more powerful than our body because it can make our body irrelevant.

On June 16, 1963, Buddhist monk Thich Quang Duc, who was protesting religious persecution under the Diem regime, immolated himself in downtown Saigon. After his death, his body was re-cremated, but his heart supposedly remained intact. This was interpreted as a symbol of compassion and led Buddhists to revere him as a bodhisattva, heightening the impact of his death on the public psyche. If you have ever seen the powerful footage, you will see that his body stayed in its seated posture while it was being consumed by fire. He was able to do this because he had mastered the physical world and his body by mastering his mind. The depth of purpose he felt in his soul was even more powerful than the agony of his body being burned alive.

Of course, this is an extreme example of what the mind can do for us. But to a mind that has accepted the transitory nature of life and has detached from all outcomes, cancer and everything else that happens in this world become peacefully irrelevant. Being detached in this manner doesn't mean that life is no longer enjoyable. On the contrary, if you have ever spent time with spiritual masters, you will find that they smile and laugh a lot more than the typical human being and nothing makes them giggle harder than the great drama and seriousness with which less spiritually advanced folks approach their lives.

Liberation from the world will do this for you and will often create states of bliss that are unachievable when we are bogged down by attachment. And what's even better is that these high vibration states are also our ideal healing states. By staying peaceful in cancer's presence, we simply give it less ground to take root in.

By no means am I trying to say that the level of physical suffering one can endure with cancer is something easy to overcome mentally. It is a daunting challenge but a worthy one because it can literally transform the experience of having cancer and, on an even deeper level, the experience of fear itself.

My wonderful father died of cancer, but he had a powerful religious faith that enabled him to literally detach from this world on a certain level. Sensing this, I once asked him if he was looking forward to dying and he said he was. Though he had lived a rewarding life, he felt that better things were in store than what our world had to offer him. This allowed him to get beyond this world while he was still living in it.

Ironically, this probably helped him to live longer! He got cancer when he was 65 and lived until he was 83. The deep peace and surrender he felt in his heart certainly played a role in him living so long because he never experienced the physically debilitating "disease" that most people have with the disease. This was a great lesson for me and I am forever grateful to him for providing it.

Now as I write this, my mother has lung cancer and has been in quite a bit of pain from the illness and radiation treatments. On a recent visit with her, she told me if the suffering gets much worse that she hopes she can count on me to take her to Oregon. She and I had taken great road trips in the past to the gorgeous canyon country of Utah and through Northern California and Nevada. We love exploring together and I thought this was what she was referring to. So I said, "Sure, of course" and then asked her if a road trip like that would lift her spirits.

But then she told me that was not what she had in mind. She wanted me to take her to Oregon because that's where assisted suicide is legal. Now at this point I certainly could have reacted with heaviness at the thought of this solemn trip. But as I see it, that is not my job. That would only create more heaviness for my mom. My job is to try to remove her mental suffering so her body has a better chance of getting into a healing state.

So without missing a beat I replied, "Sure, that will be great. My baggage will be a lot lighter on the way home!" This unexpected response totally surprised her and she replied, "But I won't be bringing much baggage, John!" To which I responded, "No, I mean my psychological baggage!" We both then cracked up and had a light, fun moment together, during what to most would be a potentially grave discussion.

We put her assisted suicide in a humorous context, thus giving us a way to think and talk about it in a non-fearful manner. And why shouldn't we set the agenda like this? We are the authors of our experience so it is up to us to establish the context with which we view our life and our death, not cancer. There is simply no reason to hand that power over to a disease. We always have to remember who is boss. Cancer is not who we are, so it is important to not make it our identity. It should never become "mind cancer" even if we have brain cancer.

My mother and I had another potentially deep talk about which treatment she was going to undergo. She was sounding very agitated like she thought I was going to tell her what she should do, including making a request for her to quit her 60-year-old habit of cigarette smoking. She has lung cancer, after all. But I had long before decided I wasn't going to tell her what to do. It was her decision and her decision alone. She is a very independent and strong-willed woman, and I didn't want to add to her state of agitation in any way by entering into conflict with her over her choices.

Instead, I decided that I was just going to stay by her side and walk with her, literally and figuratively, wherever her treatment and her life took her. This way she would never feel alone. Whatever she wanted to do was totally fine with me, and she would have my total support no matter what.

So when she very defensively told me that she and only she would decide what her fate would be and what treatment she would undergo, I think she expected me to fight her on it. Instead, I replied, "Mom, whatever you want to do is fine with me. If you want to go in the backyard and have a monkey drop coconuts on your head, I will support that fully." Then we both broke into hysterics. After we calmed down, she asked me if I could please send her a stuffed monkey to always remind her of what I said. I ordered it that same day. She recently told me that whenever she tells other people about our ridiculous exchange, they always bust into laughter. Humor is a powerful ally indeed.

In the end, it must always be remembered that this world is just a temporary destination along our soul's greater journey. This is the deal when we purchase our ticket so this must be accepted first and foremost. As Jim Morrison said, "No one here gets out alive." So instead of fighting this, it is far wiser to put our resources toward things we can do something about.

And whether you live for 100 years or for just a quick burp of an existence, the directive stays the same. Follow your bliss, come from love and learn as you go. This will keep you in your greatest healing state at all times and ensure that no matter what comes your way, you will make the most of it. Because what should be infinitely more objectionable than being diagnosed with terminal illness is living a life that wasn't worth living in the first place. And when used properly, there's no greater motivational speaker than cancer for getting this important point across.

Author's Note:

My wonderful mom has since transitioned out of here (lucky gal!), but I am happy to say that I got to spend the last full night of her life, lying on the floor in her bedroom, next to her bed, expressing my profound appreciation and love to her. Of course, the night would not have been complete without throwing in a few giggles about a certain monkey oncologist and a laugh-filled, mental trip to Oregon we once shared.

VOICES

Live as if you were to die tomorrow. Learn as if you were to live forever.

Mahatma Gandhi

Death is not the greatest loss in life. The greatest loss is what dies inside us when we live.

Norman Cousins

If you realize that all things change, there is nothing you will try to hold on to. If you are not afraid of dying, there is nothing you cannot achieve.

Anonymous

To die will be an awfully big adventure.

Aristotle

My father always used to say that when you die, if you've got five real friends, then you've had a great life.

Lee Iacocca

Let us endeavor to live so that when we die even the undertaker will be sorry.

Mark Twain

When death, the great reconciler, has come, it is never our tenderness that we repent of, but our severity.

T.S. Eliot

People are born for different tasks, but in order to survive every one requires the same nourishment: inner peace.

Sri Sathya Baba

The path to awakening is not so difficult for those who have no preferences.

Buddha

5
BE TOLERANT OF INTOLERANCE

The only truly good use for something negative in life is to utilize it for positive means. One way to do this is to take all the momentum a negative thing has going for it, re-contextualize it, and then get that momentum going in a different direction toward a positive resolution.

Kind of like a matador with an angry bull. But instead of stabbing the bull and trying to kill it as it charges at us, we gently redirect its energy and turn it out to greener pastures and a happier existence. Like how about an open range full of sexy female cows with lots of grass to chew on and lots of free time? I am not a bull, at least not in this incarnation, but that might be a reasonable place to start to look for bovine bliss.

Now let's say the angry bull is human intolerance. When you look out on the affairs of the world, intolerance often plays a major role in how we conduct business. Wherever there is an "us" and a "them" separated out, you see the workings of intolerance and, when you do, it's never an ideal situation. Intolerance attacks relentlessly and aims to maim and kill, just like an angry bull. If you are living in this world, unfortunately you are not immune to this. We have all been judged and have judged others, and we have certainly all been gored.

Now let's try to look at intolerance with some compassion and tolerance, and see if we can understand it a little more. Usually when a characteristic in human behavior is as primordial as intolerance seems to be, we can probably assume at one point the trait served a purpose. Looking back, it seems clear that in the beginning stages of human evolution anything that promoted separation from others helped us survive as individuals.

Perhaps as we emerged from the primordial soup, we needed to establish ourselves as viable individuals among the vast population of life forms inhabiting Earth. If we had not been able to establish a toehold in this realm, we would have quickly disappeared, never to be heard from again. To survive as individuals, we needed to become something different than the formless liquidity from whence we came.

By being discriminatory toward anything that seemed different from us, it strengthened our individuality and created a separate identity to defend and support. There was our toehold. Now if we wanted to survive outside of whatever womb we were unlucky enough to fall out of, this meant being suspicious of most anything that came our way.

If we weren't, bad things could happen. Heck, we could even get eaten, life's most enduring insult to individuality. And, since we didn't want to get eaten, we had to eat others instead, literally and figuratively. So in every encounter someone was going to feast, and someone was going to get served up. And that was that.

There was no debating these things over chocolate lattes at the mall or in the dark, short corridors of our primitive mind. It was all about what got you through the next moment and kept you alive to live (or suffer) another day. In the modern world however, like so many other vestiges leftover from early human development, intolerance no longer serves any useful purpose.

Too bad there is not a simple procedure to remove it like an "intolerancectomy." Actually, there is a way to remove it, and it doesn't require surgery because it has nothing to do with the body. It's called joining and the place we do it is in the mind.

In a world where we interact directly or indirectly with millions of other human beings over the course of a lifetime, joining is now the wisest survival skill going.

In *Ten of the Greatest Christmas Gifts Ever Given* by Rochelle Pennington, the author tells the enlightening story of the World

War I "Christmas Truce" of 1914 that demonstrates how receptivity and an open mind can rescue us even in the darkest of times.

It is estimated that roughly 100,000 soldiers experienced the unofficial truce that spanned hundreds of miles along the trenches of the Western Front on Christmas Eve and Christmas Day of that year. The soldiers were fighting in the "Great War" ("Great" for whom? Certainly not the brave soldiers stuck doing the actual fighting) that was pitting the Allied Powers of France, England, the United States, Russia, Japan and Italy against the Central Powers of Germany, Austria-Hungary, Bulgaria and the Ottoman Empire.

It was on that historic day several months into the bloody conflict that would rage for another four years, when the killing suddenly came to a surprising halt. It was after 10 p.m. on Christmas Eve, and soldiers on both sides were settling in for another hellish night.

Suffering in the cold, muddy trenches that separated the combatants by only a few yards, all they could do was wait for the next round of violence to commence and discover what their fate would become. But, in the pregnant pause of that hopelessly gloomy night, suddenly there was the most unexpected and surreal sound.

In the bloody aftermath of the day's intense fighting, someone could be heard singing. An unarmed German soldier was offering an unlikely Christmas gift, peace. Stepping alone and unarmed into the forbidding "no man's land" that divided the enemy camps, he walked out into the open singing "Stille Nacht" ("Silent Night").

He was using his life as a bridge upon which mortal enemies could come together and meet. In one brave, transcendent action, he was wiping away the deep-seated intolerance that breeds the hatred required to wage war. He was gifting his foes the chance to celebrate the holiday dedicated to "The Prince of Peace."

Inspired by the German's otherworldly act, soldiers on both sides began setting down their arms for a holiday truce. This started a chain reaction up and down the line, and for miles unarmed enemies began crawling out of their trenches so they could meet in the middle.

A soldier in a British regiment recalled a German who spoke fluent English coming across no man's land in the darkness calling out: "I am a lieutenant! Gentleman, my life is in your hands, for I am out of my trench and walking toward you. Will one of your officers come out and meet me halfway? I am halfway across now, alone and unarmed. Gentleman, I am waiting. Will not one of you come out and meet me?"

In some areas of the Western Front, enemies carried lit Christmas trees after the Germans had them transported by the thousands to the front lines. They were lit on Christmas Eve and this helped set the stage for the unexpected truce. In other areas of the front, simple white flags were waved. One soldier was seen carrying a prophetic sign which said simply: "You no fight. We no fight."

As the truce took hold, the occupants of the trenches came out and began exchanging gifts from Christmas parcels they had received from their families. Soldiers swapped cakes, plums, chocolates, sausages, mince pies and almonds. French soldiers brought out bottles of wine and champagne. Germans donated beer and schnapps. Scots opened bottles of rum. Soon one of the most unlikely celebrations the world had ever seen commenced.

The previously mortal enemies exchanged photographs of loved ones and partook in a friendly game of soccer. Soldiers from both sides worked together and held joint services to bury the dead that were spread around the battlefield.

Off in the distance church bells were heard ringing at midnight as worshippers gathered to celebrate Christmas Mass. After the war, uniform buttons, badges, belt buckles and helmets that the soldiers exchanged would be cherished mementos of this extraordinary moment of solidarity. Gustav Riebensahm, commanding a Westphalian regiment said, "One had to look again and again to believe what was happening."

A French officer summed up his thoughts in the simple words: "For an instant the God of goodwill was once more master of this corner of the earth."

Lance-Corporal Henderson of the Royal Engineers said of his experience: "We discovered a board stuck up in the German trench. We had our glasses on in a minute, and read the words in big block letters: "CONCERT OVER HERE TONIGHT. ALL BRITISH TROOPS WELCOME." The Germans were heard shouting: "No shoot tonight! Sing tonight! Sing tonight!"

A British war correspondent reported that later on in the evening the soldiers could hear a powerful, clear voice singing the beloved French carol, "O Holy Night." The singing soldier was Victor Granier, formerly of the Paris Opera.

On January 8, 1915, *The Scotsman* newspaper reported: "It was the simple impulse of human souls, drawn together in the face of a common and desperate plight. Those of us who are left at home may well think of the Christmas truce with wonder and thankfulness. The men who kept the truce proved, as men will always prove when the challenge is given with sufficient directness, that the human soul stands out, quite simply, as a thing of infinite goodwill."

When the order was given by superiors to commence firing after the truce ended, many soldiers refused to fire their weapons. Vize-Felfwebel Lange of the XIX Saxon Corps responded to the order by saying, "We can't fire, they are good fellows."

Finally, one officer turned on the men who wouldn't shoot and demanded, "Fire, or we do and not at the enemy!" No one was firing at them from the enemy camp, but finally the men relented and fired their guns. This was followed by a return volley of fire, but not a single man was hit, and for good reason. Recalled Lange, "We spent that day and the next wasting ammunition trying to shoot the stars down from the sky." Eventually, the tragic war was re-instigated and ground on for four more years.

Interestingly enough, a month before Christmas, Winston Churchill, who would later become British Prime Minister during World War II, had presciently asked, "What would happen, I wonder, if the armies suddenly and simultaneously went on strike, and said some other method must be found of settling this dispute?" His question is as relevant today as a century ago.

It is important to note also that the heroes of this shining moment were not five-star generals, prime ministers, kings, queens or presidents. It was the soldiers who were lowest in the chain of command who had the most first-hand experience of the war.

They proved that everyone has the power to put a stop to the intolerance that leads to so much of the world's suffering. That these battle-scarred warriors chose to honor the spirit of Christmas – which ideally would be the spirit of every day – amidst the death and destruction of total world war, proves it can be done anywhere, anytime. And the place to begin is our mind.

When we use our mind to put differences aside, evolution and growth are the immediate byproducts. The ego will of course try to fight this every chance it gets because it knows that coming together as one means the extinguishing of the individual self. It has endless tricks to entice us to remain separate from others; racism, prejudice, discrimination, grievances, greed, competition, nationalism, elitism, war, etc.

The ego has been at this game for a long time. It is the true master of the dualistic universe. So this means there is no reason to beat ourselves up for falling prey to its sneaky maneuverings. That just creates another form of intolerance and another ego trick, self-loathing.

Instead, when we find ourselves in our wrong mind, we just need to remember to not judge ourselves. As *A Course in Miracles* teaches, judgment of any kind only reinforces our wrong mind. It is infinitely wiser to witness ourselves without judgment because this immediately puts us back into our right mind. Therefore, all of the ego's tricks, no matter what form they take, just need to be gently forgiven and moved past.

One of quickest ways to get beyond them is to simply look with honesty at what we become when we fall for them. Intolerance brings a fearful mind, an attack personality, a predisposition for conflict and no peace. Tolerance, by comparison, brings an open mind, a warm heart, a predisposition for joining and lasting peace.

Once this is understood, it becomes clear that being an individual and being something "special" that stands apart from everybody else is actually not the most desired result for our earthly toils.

It is an isolated way of being, with the least fellowship and joy. With tolerance, on the other hand, we get to have it all, not the least of which is the cessation of hostilities in our life.

Awareness of this fact frees our mind from the control of the ego and liberates us to what we already are, at one with everything and deserving of the endless reward this realization brings forth. In a life lived at this level, we quickly recognize that there is nothing to be gained from intolerance. The separation it creates only serves to make life itself intolerable.

A century ago some courageous and enlightened soldiers gave the world a gift of lasting beauty. They demonstrated for all time the immeasurable benefits of transcending intolerance. They showed that the peak of human experience is the breaking down of defenses to arrive at a moment where we see other people on the battlefield of life as equal to ourselves, and fighting a hard struggle just as we are. And, as *A Course in Miracles* teaches, there is no holier spot on Earth than where ancient enemies forgive each other and come together as one, and an ancient hatred becomes a present love.

So today, let's tame the angry bull and become tolerant of intolerance. When we do, our wars with the world will end and everyone we meet will become our partner in peace. It will become instantly clear that intolerance is just the mistaken belief that other people's lives and interests are separate from our own. True healing comes from waking up from this illusion.

VOICES

Though all society is founded on intolerance, all improvement is founded on tolerance.

George Bernard Shaw

No loss by flood and lightning, no destruction of cities and temples by the hostile forces of nature, has deprived man of so many noble lives and impulse as those which his intolerance has destroyed.

Helen Keller

The greatest problem in the world today is intolerance. Everyone is so intolerant of each other.

Princess Diana

Intolerance is itself a form of violence and an obstacle to the growth of a true democratic spirit.

Mohandas Gandhi

Nothing dies so hard, or rallies so often as intolerance.

Henry Ward Beecher

I never will, by any word or act, bow to the shrine of intolerance or admit a right of inquiry into the religious opinions of others.

Thomas Jefferson

6

CELEBRATION IS HIGH ART

When you consider all the things that happen in this world that you can't control and don't really like, a healthy celebration represents a great victory. It makes the resounding statement that you are the boss of your life and a very effective one because you know how to be truly productive with your time. In fact, ceasing all normal productivity from time to time is one of the most productive things you can ever do. When you release your grip on the reins a bit, you actually regain control of your journey.

Whether you are celebrating a special accomplishment or you're just rewarding yourself for continuing to survive your very challenging Earth adventure, you are taking back the steering wheel of your life. Unburdened by the pressing details of your existence, those bossy passengers barking at you from the back seat of your mind, you can now drive yourself to higher elevations. And since we are all connected, your joy is joy to the world.

People often mistake the mechanics of everyday life like doing the chores, going to work, keeping up with social obligations...for the goal of life, to experience unfettered happiness. Of course, the mechanics of life are important too. And with the proper mindset, they can be rewarding as well. If you have ever seen a Zen Buddhist raking a rock garden, it is clear that mindfulness can turn any endeavor into a meaningful experience.

But it is celebration that lets you experience one of the great payoffs of being alive, the opportunity to express gratitude. Gratitude is the capital of the state of bliss, and celebration brings you to that magical state in style. This is why celebration is one of the highest of all art forms. Your canvas is your state of consciousness. Moods are your colors. Thoughts are your brush strokes. Happiness is your finished masterpiece.

Unfortunately, one of the great challenges of being human is that we also have a part of our mind that specializes in feeling guilty. But when you look a little deeper, whether or not you are experiencing guilt just comes down to a simple choice you are making. Are you looking at yourself from your right mind or your wrong mind?

Your right mind knows that everything is okay, and you are entitled to experience joy because happiness is your birthright. In other words, time to celebrate. Your wrong mind shrieks about all the mistakes you have made, all that you haven't gotten accomplished, and all the things you have to fear. In other words, time to jump off a bridge.

This has been the conscience war raging inside us probably since we first learned to think in opposites. By coming up with a good that was opposite from a bad, and a right that was opposite from a wrong, we created a psychological structure for inner turmoil.

As a result, we gave ourselves the difficult job of having to navigate through life with two minds that are in opposition to each other. This is kind of like driving down the road to happiness with the parking brake on.

The right mind is capable of celebration, joy, love, unity and transcendence. The wrong mind is capable of fear, judgment, guilt, separation and regret. As long as both continue to be propped up, peace is impossible.

Thankfully, since this conflict is inside our head and not somewhere external to us, its armistice is entirely in our hands. To reestablish peace when the negative thoughts pop up, simply observe them like clouds passing in the sky with as little attachment as possible. They are not who you are. It will help to remember that the sun is always shining brightly beyond the clouds, no matter how threatening they appear.

At first it may take some effort to train yourself to do this. But when you've finally had enough of the constant back and forth between feeling good and feeling bad and say enough is enough, a little effort will be well worth the reward it will bring. You will take back control of your mind.

Ultimately, the choice is yours. Is your life going to be a blast or is it going to be a bummer? You can have what you want, but you have to be bold enough to assume the best about yourself.

So why not experience some enduring sunshine for a change and commit to the positive? What could you possibly have to lose? Then celebrate a little and grow the muscles in your mind that lift your spirits to their proper height. These muscles will serve you for the rest of your life and, every time you use them, will deliver an empowering dose of good news.

Celebration says that no matter what is on the way, right now is perfectly okay.

Celebration says you are not going to let anything bring you down for too long and, therefore, you can raise the happiness of everyone around you. And when you can do that, you have accomplished one of the major goals of life.

So treat yourself to a massage or a comedy show or a round of golf or a sunset cruise.

Book a secret vacation, take a long walk with no time limit, take a long drive with no destination, enjoy a super-decadent dessert.

Sing opera in the shower, laugh your butt off at the grocery store, rip it up at a dance club, stay in bed all day when you're feeling great.

Thank some veterans for their selfless service, finally say hello to that big-time crush, go camping alone.

Get front row seats at a concert, write a love poem to your friends and family, volunteer your time, forgive an ancient enemy.

Turn a bug over that's stuck on its back, give a hundred dollar bill to a homeless person, meditate in an empty church.

Bare your soul in a deep conversation, tell a few strangers you love them, read no news for a week, give yourself a long, warm hug.

Or just do absolutely nothing better than you've ever done nothing before.

Because celebrations come in many forms, and it is the experiences of life, not the material objects of life, which boost human happiness most.

Today, take some well-deserved time off and do some serious celebrating. Put some of your highest art on display, the art of happiness. Then every time you have a chance to do it again, do it again. Join the party for goodness sakes. At the end of your life, you are not going to remember all the celebrations you turned down.

VOICES

Those who bring sunshine into the lives of others cannot keep it from themselves.

Sir James M. Barrie

The joy that isn't shared dies young.

Anne Sexton

One joy scatters a hundred griefs.

Chinese Proverb

Where there is joy there is creation. Where there is no joy there is no creation: know the nature of joy.

Veda Upanishads

One filled with joy preaches without preaching.

Mother Teresa

The more I think it over, the more I feel that there is nothing more truly artistic than to love people.

Vincent van Gogh

The only people for me are the mad ones, the ones who are mad to live, mad to talk, mad to be saved, desirous of everything at the same time, the ones who never yawn or say a commonplace thing, but burn, burn, burn, like fabulous yellow roman candles exploding like spiders across the stars and in the middle you see the blue center light pop and everybody goes Awww!

Jack Kerouac

7

HEAR THE SILENCE

It has been called in spiritual circles the "thunder of the meaning-less" and the "raucous shrieking of the ego." When we are feeling more charitable about our most constant companion, we call it our internal voice. I'm sure you are familiar with it. It's that unending monologue we hear inside our head, much of it without any deep purpose or meaning. Yet, day after day we pull up a front row seat and listen to it again. And, as we listen, it steals our attention away from the present moment.

Unfortunately, the challenging thing about life in a body is, well, life in a body. We gain entry into this world by taking on a body, which is the product of two other bodies which will be our hosts when we get here. Being good, dutiful hosts, our parents set out to teach us the rules of this life, which invariably are based around the body.

We have to be taught how to function in a physical world, or we won't survive. From basic body maintenance, to health and nutrition, to morals, education and subsistence, the lessons are all designed to make us more effective as individual bodies. Most of our contemplation thus becomes body-based thinking centered around the physical world, instead of spirit-based thinking centered around the realm of spirit.

The problem with this is the thing we often become most attached to in life, the body, is actually the thing that can do the least for us in terms of true, lasting happiness. Earthly pleasures are supremely delicious, and there are so many to enjoy in this captivat-ing amusement park that one could get lost in them forever.

But at some point, it must be acknowledged that it all goes away. It is all just a preview before the big show when we leave the body and continue on as spirit or mind. And folks who spend their time lost in the previews are never fully prepared for the main attraction. The easiest way for that to happen is to never turn the body-based, internal chatter off.

As many have discovered though, finding the silence using our undisciplined, over-active minds can often be a ridiculous exercise in futility. I once heard the tale of two old friends, Brent and Jake, who moved to California and tried to meditate for the first time:

BRENT: Hey, let's try meditating. We're in California now. They love doing that here.

JAKE: Okay. Cool.

Brent and Jake sit on their carpet and cross their legs and close their eyes. After a few moments, Jake opens his eyes and looks over at Brent.

JAKE: Brent, what are we supposed to meditate about?

BRENT: Nothing.

JAKE: Okay. Sounds simple enough.

They close their eyes and sit in silence for a few moments. After a short while, Jake opens one eye and looks at Brent.

JAKE: How do you meditate about nothing? You have to meditate about something or you're not really meditating, right?

BRENT: You got me. Let's meditate on it.

JAKE: Okay.

They close their eyes. After a few moments, Jake looks at Brent, confused.

JAKE: Every time I try to think of nothing, something comes in my head. Usually, when I try to think of something, nothing comes in my head.

BRENT: Well, then just do that.

JAKE: Do what?

BRENT: Try to think of something.

They close their eyes. After a few moments, Jake opens his eyes again, frustrated.

JAKE: Nothing's coming in my head.

BRENT: Me neither. Man, I had no idea meditating was so stressful. Let's go get a beer and relax!

Yes, meditating is an acquired skill and an acquired taste. But if you don't live in a cave, how in the world do you learn to silence your mind amidst the clamor of the modern world and the daily sensory overload?

Well, just like anything else, you need to grow the muscle that allows you to turn the mental faucet off. On your first attempts, it will probably seem like it is stuck in the "on" position. But by persevering amid the onslaught and dedicating just a few minutes a day to it, even if in the beginning you are totally unsuccessful, eventually it will loosen.

Even if it is for just a few seconds at first, you will experience a most profound phenomenon, a true moment of silence. Then as you get better, the moment will extend into a minute and then two minutes and then five and then 10. Not only will you experience the deeply healing peace of a still mind, which will refresh your physical being all the way down to the cellular level, you will also find that some of your best thinking occurs when you are not thinking at all. For only silence lets you hear divinity's whisper.

To gain fresh insights on your life, sometimes you must take yourself out of the picture. And in the silence between your thoughts, you will tap into the larger universal mind. This is where some of your greatest work on Earth will be accomplished and you won't even know you are doing it.

You see, the ego is a master at limitation. And the way it limits is by constantly filling your head with its commentary. Maybe it is worry about the future or regrets about the past. Or maybe it is reacting to and commenting on everything you see. Some estimate that the human brain produces anywhere from 10 thousand to 50 thousand thoughts per day, and the grand majority of them are repeated thoughts so it is doubtful that there is an enormous amount of innovation taking place.

The problem with this is it keeps your mind dialed to an internal talk radio station that delivers you 24/7 news about things that aren't all that important. It keeps you hooked on the mundane subject matter it specializes in and leaves no room for inspiration to have its say.

It fills your life with content that will never fully satisfy and never stop completely. It will just be the same show over and over again with no end in earshot. Inspired simply means "in spirit" so listening to body-based thinking by definition can never be inspirational.

On the other hand, if you want to experience something that transcends your life as a body, then you must tune your mind to divinity's station. Luckily, it doesn't require any special type of antenna or high-speed connection. It doesn't require some cosmic boom box or for you to move to a special part of the world or convert to a special religion that grants you divine reception.

Every soul on Earth is born with the built-in connection needed to get this transcendent transmission silent and clear. You just need to start turning off the world and start dialing up some silence.

Once you start receiving the benefits of its quiet power and the gift of inspiration it brings, you will realize there is no sound on Earth more beautiful or more natural. As the Zen teacher Adyashanti points out, "True meditation is just accepting things as they truly are." In silence, this becomes automatic.

As you learn to cultivate it, you will come to understand that silence is the backdrop to everything. It heals because it is home. In fact, silence is homecoming.

So, though you may seem to have wandered off and found yourself in a world filled with endless chatter, your true home is safe and awaiting your return. The only way to get there is the mind. Just follow the silence.

VOICES

To a mind that is still the whole universe surrenders.

Lao Tzu

In an attitude of silence the soul finds the path in a clearer light, and what is elusive and deceptive resolves itself into crystal clearness.

Mahatma Gandhi

Nothing is more useful than silence.

Menander of Athens

See how nature – trees, flowers, grass – grows in silence; see the stars, the moon and the sun, how they move in silence...we need silence to be able to touch souls.

Mother Teresa

Silence is as deep as eternity: speech, shallow as time.

Thomas Carlyle

Silence is the universal refuge, the sequel to all dull discourses and all foolish acts, a balm to our every chagrin, as welcome after satiety as after disappointment.

Henry David Thoreau

8

LOVE BEING

What exactly are you?
When you strip away everything that is impermanent in your life, what exactly is left? What is it that endures? What is truly worth the investment of your time and energy?

To me these need to be the first questions with which you start each day, even before you open your eyes and get out of bed. Because when you dig down to the answer to this important inquiry and the core, unchanging essence of what you truly are, you will come to some very liberating realizations.

For instance, you are not your career.
You are not your job title.

You are not your politics.
You are not your worldview.

You are not your pain.
You are not your sickness.

You are not your regrets.
You are not your fears.

You are not your home.
You are not your possessions.

You are not your credit rating.
You are not your bank account balance.

You are not your greatest victory.
You are not your proudest moment.

You are not your biggest defeat.
You are not your greatest embarrassment.

You are not your height.
You are not your weight.

You are not the thickness of your hair.
You are not the size of your muscles.

You are not your nationality.
You are not your skin color.

You are not your IQ.
You are not your genetic make-up.

You are not your weaknesses.
You are not your addictions.

You are not your anger.
You are not your guilt.

You are not your age.
You are not your sex.

You are not your education level.
You are not the neighborhood you live in.

You are not your awards.
You are not your press clippings.

You are not your family history.
You are not your reputation.

In fact, you are not even the you that you think you see in the mirror each day.

All these things go away.

What is lasting is what you are right now and forever, a love being. It seems blissfully obvious, doesn't it? Haven't you ever noticed how nothing feels better, restores peace faster and heals more deeply than love, especially unconditional love?

(Don't be too fooled by conditional love. It actually isn't very loving at all. When conditions change, prepare to duck because conditional hate could be on the way!)

The reason nothing feels better than love is because that is what you are, a love being. This means you are not just the love in your heart, you *are* love. And when you are feeling the deep, healing peace of unconditional love, you are in your natural state. When you experience this, I believe you get a glimpse of what divinity feels like.

Now I'm not talking about the moody, vengeful divinities that humankind has been concocting since the beginning of recorded history. Take a survey of the world's belief systems and you'll find some pretty scary "higher beings" foraging about in the dark corners of humanity's self-concept.

Gods like these make it easy to understand why there are atheists and agnostics in the world and a lot of fearful people. The selection at The Divinity Bar doesn't always inspire confidence. Original sin for appetizer, "Planet Conflict" for the main course, eternal hell for desert? What prankster cooked up this booby prize of an existence anyway? We did, it seems. In our minds.

But this is to be expected when mortals create Gods. Lacking optimism and true spiritual vision, we design them in our own image because it is the material we know best. So instead of coming up with something transcendent that will lift us out of the clutch of earthly affairs, we just produce something very human.

We sign ourselves up for a repeat of what's been happening in the earthly realm since time began, but now it's not just humans being unforgiving toward humans. The Gods are now too. If life under these merciless conditions were a voluntary theme park ride, there would probably be no one standing in line except maybe those suffering from some form of guilt.

Seems to me, if we are going to put our faith in a higher being, why not at least make it a loving being? Strip away all the theology and it just seems to make sense, especially considering nothing feels better than love. So why not pray to that?

My so-called God is love because everything I have learned from this world tells me love, the unconditional kind, is the best thing going. So when I close my eyes to join with divinity, I no longer ask for anything specific. That would make my love conditional. Instead, I just focus on unconditional love. I quiet my mind and join in love with all that is. Who needs anything specific when you can have it all? It is so much simpler this way.

Yes, my God is love because if you are created from love then you get to be a love being, the most joyful form of life. When you are a love being, you are at peace because of what you are, not because of what you do or have.

When you are a love being, the world responds most favorably to you because the world is filled with love beings, even if a few folks that might be having a rough time at life don't fully realize it. When you are a love being, all the effort in finding happiness goes away because love is happiness and requires no effort. It's just what it has always been, forever unchanging and accessible to all.

Today, try on a new Self-definition, one that connects with all that is transcendent in life. Make love your belief system, and take a loving view on what you think you really are. Start living today as a love being and, from this day forward, you will love being alive.

VOICES

The love we give away is the only love we keep.

Elbert Hubbard

We can cure physical diseases with medicine, but the only cure for loneliness, despair, and hopelessness is love. There are many in the world who are dying for a piece of bread, but there are many more dying for a little love.

Mother Teresa

Saving love doesn't bring any interest.

Mae West

In dreams and in love there are no impossibilities.

Janos Arany

A heart that loves is always young.

Gaelic Proverb

We are not held back by the love we didn't receive in the past, but by the love we're not extending in the present.

Marianne Williamson

9
GROW STRONG IN YOUR
DISCOMFORT ZONES

As if teen angst, raging hormones, pimples, bad hair and braces weren't already challenging enough, when I turned 15, to top it all off, I got my first of many cluster headaches.

If you are not familiar with them, and I really hope you're not, cluster headaches are like super-condensed migraines that have the additional audacity to come in large bunches. In my case, a typical cluster consisted of anywhere from 40 to 60 headaches and lasted two to three months.

Each cluster would start slowly, maybe one headache every three or four days. Then the headaches would strike more frequently, eventually reaching a peak of one every day, sometimes two. This level of frequency would go on for many weeks before they would finally begin to taper off again.

Shortly after I was diagnosed with them, a doctor told me that the American Medical Association had classified cluster headaches as one of the worst pains known to humankind, even worse than childbirth, according to the few unlucky ladies who had experienced both. Needless to say, this was not good news. But it wasn't nearly as bad as when he then told me there was no real known cure either.

Each headache, or torture session as I came to see them, lasted four to five hours, and sometimes they could last all day. On bad years, I would get two clusters, or a total of 80 to 120 headaches.

Life during these cycles was nothing more than an excruciating endurance test.

Happiness quickly faded, and a sense of dread took over. Since the headaches could come at any time and destroy any moment no matter how auspicious, they gave me the gnawing fear that I had no real control of my life. That fear was with me every day because I never knew when they were going to reappear. This was when I first started to get in touch with the meaning of despair.

Since I had never met anyone else who had cluster headaches, I could never understand why only I got them. I couldn't figure out what I did wrong, but I was sure I did something pretty bad to deserve them, like maybe operating a guillotine in a past life? And then, with no more thought than that put into the most serious medical problem of my young life, I settled in for 16 long years of suffering.

The pain was mind-blowing. It literally took my breath away at times. It felt as if someone was drilling to the surface of my head from the inside, using a rusty, corroded drill bit. Only they never hit the surface. They just drilled and drilled and drilled, probing, looking for an opening, driving me mad.

When I felt the first twinge of pain each year representing the onset of another cluster of headaches, it was as if someone had turned down the dimmer switch on my life. A familiar darkness would descend on me as I once again was forced into my own private hell. I knew I was in for a two-to-three-month ride in which I would somehow have to remain productive and sane while I endured the ferocious onslaught.

The headaches frequently brought me to the edge of panic. I would often wonder if my skull would literarily explode, and often half-hoped it would to put me out of my misery. My vision would blur, and my eyes would tear and turn an unhealthy shade of deep red.

I would search for breaks in the pain and try to make them last longer through force of will. But any attention put on the headaches only made them stronger. Kind of like when someone tells you not to think of a purple elephant, and suddenly it is all you can think of.

Somehow I always made it through though, with my only reward being I then got to wait until the next one came. During class? During a work meeting? During a college final? During a date? During the middle of the night? During a vacation? They were called "suicide headaches" because that was what they literally drove people to. They were the curse of my adolescence and young adulthood.

And I am so glad I had them.

It was the headaches that first drove me to spiritual books in search of a different way to process my life and my suffering. It was the headaches that made my life so unbearable in its current form that it made me look for something more. It was the headaches that led me to seek deeper guidance and to come across the wisdom that made me realize ultimately the headaches came from me. It was the headaches that made me realize that I was not being acted on by some external force. I was acting on myself.

Over the years, I tried many approaches to deal with the pain. Cold was useless, although that didn't stop me from holding thousands of ice cubes up to my forehead. My fingers always froze, as did my forehead. The headaches did not.

Digging my finger deep into my temple could provide a momentary diversion. Taking toxic steroids and powerful painkillers and then becoming dependent on them only made me feel groggy and depressed (Demerol) and edgy and irritable (Prednisone). Moaning like it was the end of the world felt therapeutic but never was any help with the pain.

The only thing that really worked was when out of desperation, I turned to spiritual teachings, Buddhism in particular, and learned to become more mindful of my mental states. Because headaches, it turns out, are just "mindaches" in disguise.

I first became aware of this when I realized I didn't need to have a headache to have a headache. In other words, headaches come in many forms. Eventually, I figured out that everybody gets cluster headaches. I wasn't special. Other people just call them different names: regret, worry, stress, spastic colon, anxiety attacks, ulcers, back pain, insomnia. They are all headaches in a sense.

Actually, what they really are, are mindaches, the result of not treating your mind like the holiest of all temples.

When I first started to witness my state of mind with the guidance of spiritual teachers, I realized a shocking thing. I was in control of it. I also realized that it is impossible to cure physical ailments for long unless the mind is on board. In fact, when the mind is truly healed, the body no longer even matters. It can be in pain. It can be in bliss. It can live to a 100. It can die young. It is not who you are, no matter how much it demands otherwise with aches, pains, bumps and bruises.

In my case, it was forgiveness that became the great healer of my mind – forgiving the world, forgiving everyone in my life, forgiving myself, and ultimately, forgiving the headaches. I taught myself that how they were perceived was in my hands. They could only truly hurt me if I allowed them to.

By taking responsibility for the headaches and my reaction to them, I began to grow strong in my discomfort zone. I turned what had been a failure of self-awareness into a learning opportunity. Eventually, I came to see the headaches as bells of mindfulness that would wake me immediately to my poor psychological condition. If I addressed the underlying mental state, the headaches ceased to matter.

I came to understand that when they came it was because they were invited by me. Once I figured that out, it was simply a matter of sending out no more invitations. I did this by managing my mental state with the care and total commitment it deserves.

It took work, but eventually the headaches had no more ground to take root in. After 16 years, when they finally went away, I knew that they didn't leave on their own. I made them go away. And that realization is what keeps them away.

Today, take a look at the headaches and mindaches in your life and listen to what they are telling you. Better yet, listen to what you are telling you. And remember, a good struggle will strengthen you in ways lounging by the pool never will. So don't fight your discomfort zones. Work with them and see what hidden gems they are offering you. Be open to the gifts they bring and, before long, not only will you grow stronger in your discomfort zones, you will grow comfortable with them as well.

VOICES

If there is no struggle, there is no progress.

Frederick Douglass

Need and struggle are what excite and inspire us; our hour of triumph is what brings the void.

William James

Success is not measured by what you accomplish, but by the opposition you have encountered, and the courage with which you have maintained the struggle against overwhelming odds.

Orison Swett Marden

God will not look you over for medals, degree or diplomas, but for scars.

Elbert Hubbard

Life's challenges are not supposed to paralyze you, they're supposed to help you discover who you are.

Bernice Johnson Reagon

Character cannot be developed in ease and quiet. Only through experience of trial and suffering can the soul be strengthened, vision cleared, ambition inspired, and success achieved.

Helen Keller

Smooth seas do not make skillful sailors.

Proverb

10

Even In Great Numbers, We Are All One

Despite all the incredible beauty they serve us each day on their golden optical platter, our eyes often are a very bad influence. The reason for this is that they are experts at detecting differences between people. They are masters at pinpointing exactly what makes other people different from us and what separates this person from that person.

"That guy has tiny ears."
"That guy has enormous feet."
"That guy looks like a saint."
"That guy looks like a criminal."
"That guy has perfect teeth."
"That guy has a crooked nose."
"That guy has a huge forehead."
"That guy has sexy eyes."
"That guy dresses to impress."
"That guy dresses for less."
"That guy's black."
"That guy's white."
"That guy's chiseled."
"Is that guy pregnant?"

Our eyes give us bad advice because they present us with a world of separate objects, a world of separate people and therefore, a world of separate interests. They get so stuck on the superficial level of form that they often prevent us from going deeper to the level of spirit or mind where bodily differences don't exist.

Our eyes mislead us because the representation of reality they bring us is incorrect. Not only is it incorrect, it often breeds insecurity and fear. Who really wants to be a solitary individual, pitted against seven billion other solitary individuals in an often unforgiving and competitive world? Talk about another good reason to stay in bed.

There is so much more strength and reward in focusing on what unites us, rather than what divides us. But it takes a different kind of vision to see that. A simple parable from the past demonstrates this point:

"There was once a man named Ashok who had five sons who used to quarrel endlessly. Soon Ashok became fed up with his sons' fighting. One day, he gathered five dry branches and gathered them into a bunch and told his sons, 'Who ever will break this bunch of branches will get ten rupees from me.'

"One by one, all of them tried to break the bunch, but none could succeed. Ashok then opened the bunch and gave one branch to each son. He asked them again to break the branch they now held and all could do so easily.

"Ashok told his sons, 'When the branches were together none of you could break them but, when they were separated you could break them easily. Similarly, if you will live in unity, you will be much stronger than if you live as individuals. In fact, your bond will be unbreakable.' From that day forward Ashok's sons stopped quarreling amongst themselves and lived in peace."

Then there is this modern tale about the power of unity, *A Head with a Heart,* told beautifully by Kevin Cullen on March 12, 2009 in *The Boston Globe.*

"Paul Levy, the guy who runs Beth Israel Deaconess Medical Center, was standing in Sherman Auditorium the other day before some of the very people to whom he might soon be sending pink slips. In the days before the meeting, Levy had been walking around the hospital, noticing little things.

"He stood at the nurses' stations, watching the transporters, the people who push the patients around in wheelchairs. He saw them talk to the patients, put them at ease, make them laugh. He saw that the people who push the wheelchairs were practicing medicine.

"He noticed the same when he poked his head into the rooms and watched as the people who deliver the food chatted up the patients and their families.

"He watched the people who polish the corridors, who strip the sheets, who empty the trash cans, and he realized that a lot of them are immigrants, many of them had second jobs, most of them were just scraping by.

"And so Paul Levy had all this bouncing around his brain the other day when he stood in Sherman Auditorium.

"He looked out into a sea of people and recognized faces: technicians, secretaries, administrators, therapists, nurses, the people who are the heart and soul of any hospital. People who knew that Beth Israel had hired about a quarter of its 8,000 staff over the last six years and that the chances that they could all keep their jobs and benefits in an economy in freefall ranged between slim and none.

"I want to run an idea by you that I think is important, and I'd like to get your reaction to it," Levy began. "I'd like to do what we can to protect the lower-wage earners – the transporters, the housekeepers, the food service people. A lot of these people work really hard, and I don't want to put an additional burden on them.

"Now, if we protect these workers, it means the rest of us will have to make a bigger sacrifice," he continued. "It means that others will have to give up more of their salary or benefits.

"He had barely gotten the words out of his mouth when Sherman Auditorium erupted in applause. Thunderous, heartfelt, sustained applause.

"Paul Levy stood there and felt the sheer power of it all rush over him, like a wave. His eyes welled and his throat tightened so much that he didn't think he could go on.

"When the applause subsided, he did go on, telling the workers at Beth Israel, the people who make a hospital go, that he wanted their ideas. The lump had barely left his throat when Paul Levy started getting e-mails.

"The consensus was that the workers don't want anyone to get laid off and are willing to give up pay and benefits to make sure no one does. A nurse said her floor voted unanimously to forgo a 3 percent raise. A guy in finance who got laid off from his last job at a hospital in Rhode Island suggested working one less day a week. Another nurse said she was willing to give up some vacation and sick time. A respiratory therapist suggested eliminating bonuses.

"I'm getting about a hundred messages per hour," Levy said yesterday, shaking his head.

"Paul Levy is onto something. People are worried about the next paycheck because they're only a few paychecks away from not being able to pay the mortgage or the rent.

"But a lot of them realize that everybody's in the same boat and that their boat doesn't rise because someone else's sinks.

"Paul Levy is trying something revolutionary, radical, maybe even impossible: He is trying to convince the people who work for him that the E in CEO can sometimes stand for empathy."

Yes, when you consider all the enormous challenges that life presents us with like recessions, natural disasters, famines and the like, it just makes so much more sense to pull together and join as one. Not just in body, because that's not always possible in this realm, but in mind.

This is not a new proposal, of course. It has been the suggestion of great spiritual teachers throughout history dating all the way back to antiquity, folks who were able to use spiritual vision to see beyond the world of form to the deeper level where we are all one.

In the modern world, there is now a whole new group of unity advocates. Quantum physicists confirm through an entirely different way of seeing that the physical universe filled with separate objects is but an optical illusion. There is no here and there because there is actually here, and everything is connected. They confirm what enlightened sages from thousands of years ago first spoke about in sacred Hindu texts.

Scientists who study plants have also confirmed the interconnectedness of all things. When they wire plants to galvanometers, they are able to record electric potential and basic charge fluctuations. To their astonishment, they are able to demonstrate that plants read and react to human beings' states of mind. They are sometimes more in tune with us than some of our human counterparts. Plants have even been used as lie detectors.

According to extensive experiments detailed in the illuminating, paradigm-shifting book, *The Secret Life Of Plants* by Peter Tompkins and Christopher Bird, plants experience severe distress not only when humans mutilate or damage them, but also when humans just *think* about mutilating or damaging them. They also grow healthy and strong when they are admired and spoken to in a nurturing manner. In return, they are calming and healing to humans and have wedded themselves to us in complex, bio-chemical relationships.

So, not only do they beautify our world, give us oxygen to help us breathe, provide us medicines and fill our stomachs with delicious, healthy meals, they are also more like domesticated pets than senseless automatons. Aristotle even believed they have souls.

This seems to be a much more uplifting reason to take care of the environment than the doom and gloom scenarios put forth to make us live in harmony with the Earth. Just think of every plant and tree you see as the family dog or cat and suddenly recycling and cleaning up our planet feels less like an obligation and more like an expression of love to our green, leafy friends.

But, even more important than the environmental ramifications of this research, the apparent connection between plants and animals speaks to a medium that connects us all in ways that our eyes and physical senses may not be able to perceive, but that nonetheless is very real.

The universe, after all, means "one verse" or "one song" and when we all sing together, harmony is assured. If we have any doubts about this, then we simply need to try on a unity headspace and see how great it feels.

Spend this day looking for shared interests and things you have in common with others. Let their individual, bodily traits fall away and envision instead the deeper fabric that ties you together with them. Maybe it is spirit. Maybe it is energy. Maybe it is white light. Maybe it is love. Or maybe it is the mind. Whatever the bridge is that ends up connecting you to others, start building it. For what awaits at the connecting point is true reality.

Take a unity headspace out for a spin and let that be your vantage point instead of the body that we all love to sport our individuality in. The second your eyes try to tell you someone is different from you, and has interests separate from your own, use your heart and your mind to re-establish common ground.

Even if it sounds totally counterintuitive, forget yourself and gain the whole world. You will come out way ahead in the exchange. And the way you will know is the deep peace you will experience.

One of the reasons religions hold such sway in our world is because in their purest form they have the ability to put us in touch with something bigger than ourselves. Nothing in the material world, despite what all the glossy commercials tell us, can compare with the experience of cosmic consciousness where walls of separation come down and the unity of all things is revealed.

Saints that ascend to these beatific states don't do it by standing in the middle of the world surrounded by billions of individuals and proclaiming their specialness. They don't do it by being extra-attached to the world and trying to become the greatest spiritual teacher of all time. They do it by surrendering the concept of "me." In the end, "me" is actually not the most advantageous way to think of ourselves. All it gets us is "me." "We," on the other hand, is limitless.

In a truly transcendent moment, which is the natural resumption of communion with all that is, a different type of perception takes over. We don't see differences anymore. We realize that the grand spectacle of life on Earth and the vast play of individual existences and individual bodies is just a glorified costume party.

The impermanence of it all becomes undeniable evidence that it is a show and not ultimate reality. When we lose our infatuation with this fleeting individuality, we're then free to experience the greatest feeling of love in the entire world, a sense of oneness with all things.

A few sips of this ascendant nectar and it quickly dawns on our minds that true love is not what we feel for objects of our fancy. True love is not an item of exchange, to be given and then retracted based on circumstance or mood. That is conditional love. True love is what we are, indivisible from all that is, forever unified with all living beings in peace. There is no sweeter realization in life.

Today, live this day in your mind as if you are joined with all that is. Because the second you do, you will be. That's the miraculous thing about the mind. It doesn't let a temporary limitation like the body get in the way of a perfect thing.

VOICES

Tis better to plumb the depths of unity than forever scratch the surface of variety.

Emile Zola

The reason why the world lacks unity, and lies broken and in heaps, is because man is disunited with himself.

Ralph Waldo Emerson

Behold how good and how pleasant it is for our brethren to dwell together in unity.

Bible

If one pulls on a single thread in nature, you'll find it attached to everything else.

John Muir

A human being is a part of a whole, called by us – universe - a part limited in time and space. He experiences himself, his thoughts and feelings as something separated from the rest... a kind of optical delusion of his consciousness. This delusion is a kind of prison for us, restricting us to our personal desires and to affection for a few persons nearest to us. Our task must be to free ourselves from this prison by widening our circle of compassion to embrace all living creatures and the whole of nature in its beauty.

Albert Einstein

11

HUMANITY IS MY HOME TEAM

W hen the relationships between nations seem too complex to
sort out, and life on Earth feels like one, big, geopolitical
family feud, it is wise to keep in mind that national borders are just
figments of our imagination. When boiled down to their essence,
they are just one of the many tools the ego uses to maintain a world
of separation and division.

A *Course in Miracles* teaches that the ego is simply a fearful
thought that comes from the wrong mind, which is essentially the
fearful mind. One simply needs to understand its purpose so as not
to fall prey to its tireless maneuverings. An ego thought has one
goal, to protect the ego's individuality and ensure its survival.

Only in a world of separate entities do egos maintain their
power and have any impact on the proceedings. In perfect oneness,
egos cease to exist. So the ego makes its living convincing people
that they have individual interests separate from everyone else's.
Nation states are just an extension of this mechanism.

In our world, people get intensely wrapped up in nationalism
and patriotism. This gives them the need to designate their country as the best and the one God is actually behind. But, when you
think about it, who in their right mind would want a God that plays
favorites?

We see this same tendency demonstrated in sports. It has
become pretty common to see athletes thanking God for their victories over the poor sap on the other side who obviously has no God
rooting for him. In the process, they put their God on the level of

the average sports fan, sitting up in heaven with a beer and a hot dog glued to his big-as-the-universe, plasma TV.

Athletes do it after home runs, touchdowns, goals, or when they win a boxing match by separating the other boxer from his senses. With their foe bloody and brain-damaged at their feet, they look up to the heavens and offer their gratitude. It is certainly wonderful that they display humility and the recognition that whatever we do, we don't do alone. But sometimes we have to look a little deeper to see what our thinking and our prayers are really asking for.

That's why one of the greatest moments in sports is when the contest is over, and the competitors come together and shake hands. It feels so healing to watch walls come down and see people join. Too bad we can't fast-forward the world to the end of the competition where we could all come together, shake hands and join as one.

Because when the tendency to win at all costs reaches the level of nation states, things become much more problematic. What is usually not realized is that when we over-indulge in patriotism, we actually degrade the world in which our nation resides.

By demoting all the other countries in the community of nations below ours so we can declare our country number one, it means the community of nations itself is degraded. So in its elitism, a country actually proves it is not elite. How elite can a nation be if it merely dominates a second-rate world filled with second-class nations? How elite can a nation be if it relishes putting down other nations in the first place?

I remember when 9/11 occurred. It was a heartbreaker on so many levels. It increased the suffering in the world. It increased the distrust. It increased the hatred. It strengthened the division between nations, religions and different ways of life.

Plus, it increased patriotism and flag waving. As an American who loves our country deeply for all the good it tries to do in the world, I found that profoundly moving.

It just would have been reassuring to see another flag waved along with the American flag, a world flag, because the only lasting victory is when the whole world wins. Real victories have nothing to do with beating our competitors, whether they are other individuals, teams, companies or countries. The only true victory comes when we realize that, on a deeper level, everybody is on the same team. The end of the competition is the only victory with any lasting meaning.

I once had a discussion with a friend about what the greatest gift an alien invasion would bring. We agreed that, at least for that moment, perhaps humans across the world could finally pull together and be on the same team for the first time in history. It would probably take the potential annihilation of the human race to do it though. But it would almost be worth it to feel the power of a unified Earth.

So where does it all end? In the mind, the only place the problems of the world can truly be remedied. So there is no need to wait for the UN or religion or capitalism or government or any particular lifestyle to unify the world. There is also no need to start scanning the night skies for alien visitors to arrive and suddenly unite us all. Just look to your mind. As the timeless spiritual teaching so clearly points out: "Change the way you look at the world and the world you look at changes."

Today, make the decision deep down that "humanity is my home team" and wrap yourself in an invisible flag that bears this message. With this perspective, you will now have the whole world to root for, and you can't imagine how many more victories you will get to celebrate because of this subtle change of mind. In fact, it is the subtle change of mind itself that is the greatest victory of all.

VOICES

Where there is unity there is always victory.

Publilus Syrus

I know that my unity with all people cannot be destroyed by national boundaries and government orders.

Leo Tolstoy

The unity of freedom has never relied on uniformity of opinion.

John F. Kennedy

What ever beauty may be, it has for its basis order, and for its essence unity.

Father Andre

Remember upon the conduct of each depends the fate of all.

Alexander The Great

You can't shake hands with a clenched fist.

Indira Gandhi

There is an energy field between humans. And, when we reach out in passion, it is met with an answering passion and changes the relationship forever.

Rollo May

The main ingredient of stardom is the rest of the team.

John Wooden

12

LET GO TO GET A BETTER GRIP

From the moment we enter the world to the day we transition out, we cling for survival. If mom or dad leaves for too long, a newborn baby will raise such a perfect ruckus it can compel its fully-grown adult parents to drop everything and come running.

Early on, a baby learns to make itself miserable when it doesn't get what it needs because when it expresses that misery the world responds favorably. In reacting to an unexpected turn of events, its own birth, the baby has stumbled on a survival strategy: "Demand and you will receive." And we certainly can't blame a baby for its life-saving ad lib.

One moment it is floating in a warm cocoon connected to a non-stop buffet line of life giving nourishment. The complexity of being in a separate body has not entered the picture yet. There are no chores or any personal grooming to do. There are no thoughts of existential despair.

There is no need to build up faith in the interconnectedness of all things because its very living arrangement confirms this. It feels at one with its creator because it is at one with its creator. The idea of perfect oneness has not been shattered.

Indeed, life will never get more psychologically chill than this. So there is no hurry to do anything but enjoy its seeming good fortune, to whatever extent it understands it. But then just when it is has gotten comfortable, the eternal trickster of life, change, announces its presence.

Suddenly the baby starts getting squeezed through an uncomfortably small opening, like a sumo wrestler going caving. To its severe distress, it slowly gets pushed and pulled against its will right out of the womb, the most comfortable home it will have in its lifetime.

It is then unceremoniously dumped out into a chilly, alien world, full of hard objects that press unnaturally against its...hey what's this, a body? What a way to get the news that you now have a cold-sensitive bodysuit welded around your mind.

Naturally the baby has no clue what to do and has only a limited set of reactions to choose from. So it instinctively opens its mouth and wails. In case everyone in the room is talking on their cell phone or texting and didn't notice, the baby squeezes blood to the surface of its face and pours salty water out of its eyes. In a lifetime of dramatic outbursts, this is the first of many. And what a debut it is. Success! A standing ovation.

But then it starts to sink in. Suddenly the baby can feel things or, more accurately, it can feel the lack of things that used to character-ize its previous home. Like warmth, food, quiet and a perpetual rest room. What's a baby to do, faced with such a rude awakening? Well, considering there are just a few buttons on the behavioral remote control, hit them all. Cry, scream and turn red!

Hungry? Cry and you will get fed. Scared? Scream and you will get picked up and warmly reassured that everything is okay. Angry? Turn red and you will be stroked until your normal color returns. And so begins the unlearning of our previous bliss state and the indoctrina-tion into the behaviors that will help us survive in our new realm.

The hardware that is the brain has now been given the software program that will run it: "Demand and you will receive." When we are rewarded for this behavior by our loving, well-meaning parents, we become masters at it. So we quickly create more things to cling to. To keep pace with our growing needs, our tactics become more sophisticated. Eventually they become so refined and imbedded that we are no longer running the program. The program is running us.

So in essence we spend our adult lives run by a software pro-gram launched by infants. But its name should really be changed to "Demand and you will be deceived" because it isn't all it is cracked up to be.

The first clue comes when we get older and get out on our own. This is when it hits us that our parents are no longer the ones who come charging when our clinging demands a response. We now have to be. But even knowing we are now responsible for filling our needs still doesn't stop us from creating more needs to fill. It is just not that easy to reverse a lifetime of programming. Besides, we're adults now and we can do what we want, right?

So eventually we cling to everything that is important to us, including the most gargantuan of all clings, outcomes. Before we know it, most every aspect of our lives is based on need. We can no longer just be. Now we have to need too.

But, if we can step out of the need-machine we have turned ourselves into for just a moment, we will soon realize that the very thing that kept us alive as newborns now deadens us as adults. Because now we are addicted to the one thing that will never satisfy us, the habit of clinging. And whatever our habits are, for all intents and purposes, we are.

The assumption to this type of life is that external things can bring us lasting happiness. Unfortunately, this is to live life based on a falsehood. The fact that the program our mind is running is telling us otherwise is ultimately irrelevant. It is up to us to shed this way of thinking.

So what do we do about this troubling tendency to cling?

Nothing. Observe it and don't judge it. Then surrender it and let it go. Simply pull the supports out from underneath it by not being attached to it one way or the other. By simply observing, you will start to relocate your center of happiness from outside your mind to inside your mind. In this moment of liberation, you will uncover nuggets of truth that have been buried under your mountain of needs all along.

Freedom is not getting what you need. Freedom is not needing anything.

Evolution is not about attaining more. Evolution is about being happier with less.

You will continue life as before, but now you will get to live without your suffocating demands stealing your joy. Now you can be fully available for the present moment, which is the best way to affect the future in a positive manner anyway.

Today, take a precious moment of your time and put it to its most healthy use and empty your mind. Let go of all the things you've been holding on to so tightly and a truly satisfying replacement will fill the space: Peace.

VOICES

Some of us think holding on makes us strong; but sometimes it is letting go.

Herman Hesse

The greatness of man's power is the measure of his surrender.

William Booth

Self-interest is but the survival of the animal in us. Humanity only begins for man with self-surrender.

Henri Frederic Amiel

The condition of an enlightened mind is a surrendered heart.

Alan Redpath

The minimum qualifications for Grace are surrender of ego.

Sri Sathya Sai Baba

13

JESUS, MUHAMMAD, MOSES AND KRISHNA
ARE UNITED IN HEAVEN

To me, heaven is not a place.

It is a state of grace and a state of mind that derives its transcendence from the awe-inspiring knowledge of perfect oneness. It is a feeling we get when we perceive that, on the deepest level, we are all connected and there are no true differences between us. There are no individual agendas. There are no separate interests. There is nothing to be separate from. There is nothing to fear.

In this state of grace, I am you and you are me and together we enter the headspace of heaven, two becoming one, carried aloft on the wings of unity. But how does one get into this state in our modern world where billions of human beings from different cultures and different religions compete to assert their individual agendas?

There is only one way up the ladder. To experience heaven-like joy while still on Earth we have to move past the ego programming that ties us to this world and let go of everything that keeps us separate from others. We have to master the art of being in the world while not being of the world. This is when transcendence occurs. And one of the unexpected benefits of doing this is that when we learn how to transcend the world we actually become much more effective in the world.

To achieve these higher states and a feeling of unity with all human beings, we must surrender the deadest weight of life, judgment. I'm not talking about the kind of judgment we use to decide when it is safe to cross the street. I'm talking about the judgment the ego uses to condemn and look down upon all those who pray to a different God than we do or who don't believe in God at all.

To avoid falling into that trap, it is helpful to remember that to effectively judge another is impossible anyway, as demonstrated by this passage from *A Course in Miracles*:

"In order to judge anything rightly, one would have to be fully aware of an inconceivably wide range of things; past, present and to come. One would have to recognize in advance all the effects of his judgment on everyone and everything involved in them in any way. And one would have to be certain there is no distortion in his perception so that his judgment would be wholly fair to everyone on whom it rests now and in the future. Who is in the position to do this? Who except in grandiose fantasies would claim this for himself?

"Remember how many times you thought you knew all the facts you needed for judgment, and how wrong you were! Is there anyone who has not had this experience? Would you know how many times you merely thought you were right, without ever even realizing you were wrong? Why would you choose such an arbitrary basis for decision-making? Wisdom is not judgment, it is the relinquishment of judgment."

Even if we could effectively judge another, why would we want to? Even when we hold onto just one percent of our judgment, peace is impossible. For just as the smallest drop of ink darkens an entire glass of water, the tiniest bit of judgment darkens the whole of our being.

Judgment is so counterproductive that it locks us out of the mental state of heaven. What could be worse? The material world and the mental state of heaven are mutually exclusive states. We can't have both, and the only one that determines where we will spend our time is us.

Every time we assert our individuality instead of unity, and separate interests instead of shared interests, we are building another addition to our home in the material world. Unfortunately, we will never reach the mental state of heaven this way.

In fact, judgment is so effective at keeping us separated from each other that the followers of some of the greatest avatars to walk the Earth, those saintly folks who spoke most eloquently about how to get in touch with our Higher Self, are often at war! Imagine what the saints who inspired these followers would think if they came back today? They would have to start all over from the beginning.

But this is what happens when we create our own exclusive Gods and establish our own exclusive contracts with the divine. In essence, we define divinity by attempting to erect a fence around the infinite. We then proceed to have murderous border wars over the imaginary boundaries we have created, condemning others for not seeing things from our exact point of view.

In our attempt to get closer to God and secure heaven for ourselves, we inevitably leave others out. But, as long as anyone is left out, heaven is unattainable. Approaches like this prove only one thing, that we are coming solely from the ego. And no matter how well-developed its theology is, the ego only leads us back to planet Earth.

All we have effectively done is sentence ourselves to a place that bears no resemblance to heaven, a place where Jesus, Muhammad, Moses, Krishna or their followers cannot possibly unite. This world, or more accurately, the thinking behind this world, won't allow it. The sad story of humanity thus becomes, to quote Shakespeare's Macbeth, "a tale told by an idiot, full of sound and fury, signifying nothing."

But the good news is that in heaven, the true unity state that we are all capable of achieving in our minds, Jesus, Muhammad, Moses and Krishna couldn't be closer. They are so close that they have dissolved into one and there is no longer any troublesome individuality to mess up a perfect thing. They are in the healing embrace of shared interests, one with all that is.

What these saints alluded to on Earth and reflected in the transcendent states they reached here, they have now become in heaven. I am not talking about the heaven in the clouds beyond some pearly gates where angels serenade us with harps and virgins serve us cherries. I'm talking about the heaven in our mind where all is one.

In the end, it is wise to remember that religions and the saints of religions are merely symbols of a higher level of truth that is impossible to put into words. As *A Course in Miracles* teaches, words are just symbols of symbols and therefore are twice removed from this ultimate reality that all religions try to express. This means there is no reason to get stuck on the details and start quarreling over how various cultures try to express what God or heaven is. That just defeats the whole purpose of the spiritual quest in the first place.

Instead, give yourself a taste of some real heaven, right here, right now. Let go of your words, definitions, categorizations, pre-conceived notions and anything else that creates separation between you and others. Open a sacred space inside of you big enough to hold the entire world in its embrace. Do this out of love and you will practice living in the only place in the world where Jesus, Muhammad, Moses, Krishna and their followers can be united forever, your mind. It's your true ticket to heaven.

Voices

He who experiences the unity of life sees his own Self in all beings, and all beings in his own Self, and looks on everything with an impartial eye.

Buddha

A man content to go to heaven alone will never go to heaven.

Boethius

The way of heaven does not compete, and yet it skillfully achieves victory.

Lao Tzu

The mind can make a heaven out of hell or a hell out of heaven.

John Milton

There are glimpses of heaven to us in every act, or thought, or word, that raises us above ourselves.

Arthur P. Stanley

14
SIMPLE IS GENIUS

Period.

15

YOUR BODY IS YOUR VEHICLE, NOT YOUR HOME

The human body is a wondrous creation. It is the most sophisticated computer on Earth, able to handle millions of jobs at once so you can have a smooth and enjoyable ride through life. It is fun to look at, fun to fall in love with, fun to feel, and fun to compete against to challenge ourselves.

It has been the subject of artists throughout the centuries. It has been the temple of religions since the beginning of recorded history.

Cities have been built for it. Highways have been paved for it. Forests have been cleared for it.

Science and medicine have been invented for it. Products and technology have been mastered for it.

The body is for many, the main object of this life, the cherished form to which so much attention is paid. We give it the star treatment and put it on a pedestal above everyone else's body in the world. We take pictures of it and check on it constantly in mirrors and most any reflection we pass. We never let it out of our sight or thoughts for long. We even bring it into our dreams and nightmares.

Because of our extreme attachment to it though, the body has become a powerful and unforgiving boss, one that threatens to make us sick and even kill us if we don't pay attention to its every need. The slightest change in it can create profound anxiety. The impact of a single gray hair is testament to the insane hold it has over our mind.

As it ages, we allow the body to extract hope from our lives and fill us with dread. It becomes a master teller of tales, weaving stories about our impending doom and how our mind's and body's fates are sealed together. It eventually turns into a ticking time bomb that slowly counts off our days until we meet our inevitable end.

Don't believe it.

You are not your body. You are the mind that is projecting your body. You are the mind that came before the body and the mind that will continue on after the body dies. This is not a new concept. It has been around for thousands of years in various spiritual traditions. But it is an idea that needs to be repeated to every succeeding generation before it gets too trapped in body-based thinking with no way out.

That's why enlightened teachers throughout the ages have repeatedly taught that the body is a projection of mind and, without a mind to project it, the body would not exist. What they are saying ultimately is that we must unlearn what our body tells us each day to find the truth.

This is a very different interpretation of reality than what many people believe. Many folks think we are born into a world that pre-dates us and outlasts us. In this scenario, we are innocent victims cast into a physical universe that is separate from us

Our body seems to be our only refuge against a threatening world that's filled with endless things that are out to get us. We must protect it at all costs because our body is our home. A foreclosure on this home, dying young, is considered the greatest tragedy of all.

Actually though, there is a rising chorus from experts and spiritual teachers from a variety of fields and eras, who say it is the other way around, that we exist before we enter the world. And I am not just referring to the millions of folks who believe in reincarnation, or the scientific evidence presented in books like Thomas Shroder's *Old Souls* that document cases of children who remember past lives down to the minutest of details.

Discoveries in more mainstream science uncovered that all interactions in nature can be described as one of four different fundamental forces: electromagnetic, weak, strong and gravitational. With further progress in quantum field studies, it was realized that these different forces are actually different aspects of one single unified field which underlies all manifestations found in the physical universe.

This unified field is the web that connects all things and is the true reality beyond the physical universe. In it, there are no separate bodies because what we perceive as separate bodies are just temporary illusions brought on by our limited perceptions. Beyond the restrictive parameters of our finite little selves is the larger Self in which all is one. This means that, despite what our senses are telling us, there is no real fundamental division into observer and observed.

Other systems of thought also refer to an unconditional, transcendent reality, what Deepak Choprah calls "a non-local intelligence or consciousness unbounded by space or time" that is the source from which the conditional, physical universe springs. In a lot of Eastern belief systems, its reality is accepted as a matter of fact, just as the multiplication table is accepted as fact in Western societies.

This universal mind is where you came from and where you are headed when this current mental projection you call your life is over. In fact, on a deeper level, you are already there. You and the universal mind are one and the same because there is only the "eternal one" in the end.

There is no second, or third or fourth or seven billionth for that matter. There only appears to be. As Gloria and Kenneth Wapnick, the great teachers of *A Course in Miracles* point out, the grand unfolding you experience as your life is actually just the thought of you being "thunk" by the larger Self.

How do we know something infinitely grander than ourselves exists and that the finite world and the finite objects within it are just products of our own limited perception? Well, the only way to really know anything is to be it (reading a book about China doesn't make us Chinese), and, while we are living in a finite body, the infinite is going to be a tough thing to get our arms around. In the meantime, we can look for clues.

For instance, without an observer, this world doesn't exist. Physics has confirmed and has the data to prove that until an observer interacts with the unified field, it remains in a state of pure undifferentiated potential, just a sea of infinite possibility. It is the act of observation that actually manifests what is being observed.

This means the universe and you came into existence together, co-stars, and co-creators in your own cosmic dance. And, when you go, the physical universe disappears to you because the real you came before the physical universe. The real you also came before this body you think is you and, once the body is gone, the real you continues on.

How could it be possible that life in a body is just a temporary sensory illusion of the mind's creation?

Well, everywhere we look there are confirmed illusions our mind creates that seem completely real. For instance, just look at how your senses work. As Kenneth Wapnick teaches, drawing from *A Course in Miracles*, you don't see with your eyes. You see with your mind. You don't taste with your tongue, you taste with your mind. You don't hear with your ears, you hear with your mind. You don't smell with your nose or feel with your fingers. It all happens in your mind.

You don't even think with your brain. You think with your mind. The brain is just the organ the mind plays to create the sensory world that you perceive. In fact, you don't even live in your body. You live in your mind. Your body is just a puppet of the mind. Take away the mind and the body doesn't even work.

Another piece of evidence that proves the mind creates illusions of stunning believability comes from our dreams. Think about when you are dreaming at night, and you actually feel someone's body in your dream. You may react to it with sweating, palpitations or even arousal. What are you feeling? The projections in your dream don't even exist. You are feeling your mind. Just like after you "wake up."

If this is all true, then what does it mean for us living in the "real world" as we like to call it? It simply means your body is your vehicle, not your home. It means you should enjoy the ride and take it out for an exhilarating, life-long spin.

Soup it up, wash it and detail it. Tour the world and experience life in it. Let it take you to school in style as you attend higher education on Earth.

But don't take it too seriously. That kills all the joy of having such an amazing set of wheels to zoom around in. The body is not what you are, so it doesn't deserve that type of heavy-handed treatment. Enjoy the heck out of it, but don't be fooled into thinking it is the end-all. It's just your rental car.

In this world, people spend enormous time and energy on their bodies and sometimes forget about where improvement is lasting, the mind. Just think of the cosmetic industry alone. In a sense, it's like drawing a pretty face in the sand and then attempting to put make-up on it between waves. No, your body is not the thing to hang your hat on.

The mind is your permanent home. So don't neglect it. Spend time there and keep it in good condition, forgiving, loving and kind. Make it the best place on Earth to park your body. But don't get too attached to the body. When its usefulness is done, simply let it go. Then enter back into your real home, the mind. It's the only thing in the whole world that lasts.

VOICES

Death is not extinguishing the light; it is only putting out the lamp because the dawn has come.

Rabindranath Tagore

Begin to see yourself as a soul with a body, rather than a body with a soul.

Dr. Wayne Dyer

Consciousness is eternal, it is not vanquished with the destruction of the temporary body.

Bhagavad Gita

You never know yourself till you know more than your body.

Thomas Traherne

Surely God would not have created such a being as man, with an ability to grasp the infinite, to exist only for a day! No, no, man was made for immortality.

Abraham Lincoln

Never put a period where God has put a comma.

Gracie Allen

16

NO NEED FOR GREED

The most incredible thing about greed, beyond the amazing lengths we go to in an effort to meet its bottomless demands, is that it never fully satisfies. Because greed is a monster that cannot be satisfied. That is what defines it. If it could be satisfied, it would be a different kind of animal entirely.

Greed is one of the great misdirection plays of the human ego. It sends our bodies scurrying off into the world thinking we will find what we believe we are missing when in actuality happiness is in the other direction, inward to the mind.

What often eludes us in our pursuit of material objects is that despite all the abundance that is associated with it, greed is actually derived from a mentality of scarcity. What keeps it going, much more than the grand acquisitions it achieves, is a feeling of incompleteness. Greed occurs when we believe we are lacking something. When this happens, we reflexively reach for something outside of ourselves to fill the void.

When we indulge in this strategy too deeply though, we start to believe the world's marketing and begin to assume that the drive to acquire is the best use of our time on Earth. It makes us feel good and what could be wrong with that, right? Materialism thus becomes a way of life and we spend our time forever on the lookout for external objects that will complete us.

The problem with this is that it makes our happiness extremely tenuous. It also makes an unflattering statement about what we believe ourselves to be. How could we be anything close to a divinely inspired being if we were created so incomplete to need so much?

How truly worthwhile can we be if all our worth is derived from material objects that will eventually fade away? After we leave the planet, is the lasting value and impact of our life only assured as long as our possessions keep circulating on the *Antiques Roadshow*?

What does it say about what is inside of us if we need so many things outside of us to make us happy? And what does it say about our reason for being alive? Were we created solely to be slaves to our reptilian lobe? If so, we better start bowing down to the nearest reptile because that is our true lord on Earth.

No, the need to acquire is not divinely inspired. Need of any sort never is. The way to know for sure is to get beyond it. Because the greatest thing about overcoming greed is that as you do, you become more and more internally wealthy. You actually learn to value yourself more by realizing you don't need anything outside yourself to be happy. This is true "wealth-consciousness."

This is why I believe the wealth-consciousness strategy regularly taught in some New Age circles seems to point us in the wrong direction if it is lasting happiness we desire. This strategy directs us to focus on getting into a mental state of "allowing" so we can attract more abundance. So according to this plan, what we *need* to do is *get* in a state of allowing to *get* the abundance we *need*.

All we are really doing is strengthening the sense of lack we feel on a deeper level. No amount of abundance will fill that void, no matter how fast we manifest more bounty to fill it. This approach also tries to spiritualize material abundance, which isn't possible, because the material world and the world of spirit are two entirely different realms.

True wealth-consciousness, on the other hand, is knowing that we are perfect and complete just as we are. Yes, we are living a challenging life that will push and pull us in many directions at once. We will need to feed ourselves and acquire certain basic items to live in a physical universe. And yes, it is important to stay in a positive state of mind because it will help to attract positive energy into our life.

We may even love to shop for luxury items from time to time to reward ourselves for all our hard work in life. There is certainly nothing wrong with that, as long as our deeper sense of core, internal worth and inherent completeness remains intact. The grandest acquisitions in the world, even those amazing Great Gatsby-class mansions that look like they could house a small village, will not bring us the type of peace of mind that comes from knowing we are perfectly fine just as we are.

Of course, it's not the size of our kingdoms that is the issue. With the proper mindset, one could live in a castle and remain non-attached. Or likewise, in a single-room, efficiency apartment. It is where we build our kingdoms that matters most. Do we erect them on the fleeting foundations of the external world, or on the permanent foundation of the mind?

There is something so classically simple and pure about Buddhist monks who can merely shut their eyes and enter their kingdom. The kind of blissful state they live in is so effortless, uncluttered and permanent. Just like truth.

Another reason it is wise to cultivate a higher sense of self than the material world offers is because the spiritual wealth this practice creates is available to everyone. There are no class differences in spiritual wealth. There are no welfare states. There are no "have-nots"...only "haves." From the most humble peasant to the richest king and queen, this type of wealth is accessible to all. And it comes in endless supply. All it takes is a proper state of mind to access it.

By realizing the inherent worth of ourselves and, by extension, all living things, we effectively break the bank and spread the wealth around perfectly. In the process, we get to join the most unexclusive community on Earth, the community of the truly rich – the spiritually wealthy – where there is no need for greed. Thankfully, since it is not a gated community everybody in the whole world is welcome. Hopefully, someday soon we will all live there together.

VOICES

People spend a lifetime searching for happiness; looking for peace. They chase idle dreams, addictions, religions, even other people, hoping to fill the emptiness that plagues them. The irony is the only place they ever needed to search was within.

Romana L. Anderson

The covetous man is ever in want.

Horace

A Native American grandfather talking to his young grandson tells the boy he has two wolves inside of him struggling with each other. The first is the wolf of peace, love, and kindness. The other wolf is fear, greed, and hatred. "Which wolf will win, grandfather?" asks the young boy. "Whichever one I feed," is the reply.

Native American Proverb

Avarice is always poor.

Samuel Johnson

Until you make peace with who you are, you'll never be content with what you have.

Doris Mortman

Earth provides enough to satisfy every man's need, but not every man's greed.

Mahatma Gandhi

You know the value of every article of merchandise. But if you do not know the value of your own soul, it is all foolishness.

Rumi

17

FAILURE PLUS LEARNING EQUALS SUCCESS

Failure can be a great success.

In fact, failure in a lot of ways is one of the best things that ever happens to us. That is, if we value evolution.

Success certainly feels wonderful and is the ultimate goal, but it's not always terribly motivating. It often tempts us to rest on our laurels and savor the victory. The great challenge of being a repeat champion in sports is testament to this. Failure though can be like a life coach's boot planted firmly on our behind.

If we think of ourselves as an engine, failure can be like rocket fuel. It can rev us up and shoot us out beyond our normal orbit into new challenges that will force us to grow and adapt. So, by failing at something, we often become more than we were before.

Over time, our failures can become the gifts that keep on giving. Down the road, if our focus falters, all we have to do is remember our failure and it is like a new burst of rocket fuel for our engine. Because the only thing more eye-opening than failing at something is failing at it again.

Failure also reminds us of why we are here, which is to learn and evolve into higher and higher states. As Friedrich Nietzsche pointed out, "He who has a why for life can put up with any how."

Failure is an invaluable part of the curriculum for a transformational, real-life education because it teaches us high-impact lessons in street smarts and helps us develop situational awareness. Situational awareness is the mental skill involved with being aware of what is happening around us so we can accurately perceive how the flow of information, events and actions impact our objectives.

According to research, inadequate situational awareness is one of the main causes of accidents blamed on human error. Isn't it reassuring to know that by making errors or failing at something, our situational awareness actually increases through the schooling we receive?

Good judgment is often the byproduct of bad experiences. That is, unless we get so guilt-ridden over the way we failed at something, like perhaps an inability to avoid a regrettable fight with someone, that we never reap the benefits of the larger lesson it holds for us, such as, "Always be kind."

By shackling ourselves with guilt, we are simply making ourselves less useful to the world. Carrying around a ball and chain like that doesn't do anyone any good. We have to assume that as long as we are still living and breathing, that improvement is our goal, not perfection.

Life is difficult enough without riding roughshod over ourselves like disapproving taskmasters. Instead, we should be our own biggest supporter at all times. That is the kindest thing we can do for the people in our life because it keeps us at our best for them. This simple adjustment transforms our mind from an enemy into an ally.

It is also wise to remember that a lot of mistakes in life work out phenomenally well in the end. And they don't have to be gargantuan. Even the tiniest mistakes can pay huge dividends.

In *Mistakes That Worked* by Charlotte Foltz Jones, the author writes about Ruth Wakefield who in 1930 worked at the Toll House Inn near New Bedford, Massachusetts. She was so busy running the inn one month it slipped her mind that she had to order more baking supplies. While mixing up a batch of her cherished chocolate cookies one day, she realized that she had run out of baker's chocolate.

As a substitute, she broke up some semi-sweetened chocolate instead. She hoped it would melt into the dough as it heated up, and she would end up with the chocolate cookies her patrons loved. But when she opened the oven, she discovered that the semi-sweet chocolate had not melted. After a couple experimental bites though, her taste buds quickly told her that she had just made a very delicious mistake. She had just invented the world's first chocolate chip cookies.

The cookies Ruth Wakefield mistakenly invented are now called "Toll House" and they are the most popular chocolate chip cookies in America. Some have estimated that seven billion chocolate chip cookies are consumed annually around the world. Think of all the tasty joy, not to mention tasty jobs, her mistake brought to the world.

In 1928, Alexander Fleming was a bacteriologist who studied germs. During an experiment at St. Mary's Hospital in London, England, he failed to put lab plates away properly that contained a deadly bacteria. Instead, he left them beside an open window. When he came back later, he found that the bacteria had been contaminated by some mold that had blown in through the window. Even though his important experiment had been destroyed, he decided to look a little deeper using a microscope.

He saw that the mold was growing on the bacteria but around it was a clear area where some of the bacteria had disappeared. He soon realized that the deadly bacteria were being dissolved by the mold. This accidental discovery led to the life-saving drug Penicillin, and an eventual Nobel Prize for Fleming and his colleagues who worked on it. You and I are probably here today because of his failure to follow proper experimental procedure.

Here are a few other things that were brought to us by mistake: tea, cheese, brown-and-serve rolls, fireworks, The Leaning Tower of Pisa, fudge, aspirin, guide dogs for the blind, X-rays, Frisbees, pacemakers, Teflon, soap, paper towels, glass, post-it notes and piggy banks.

And where would this world be without all the failures Edison experienced on his way to his huge list of inventions including the phonograph, the motion picture camera and the long-lasting electric light bulb? His failures were the unsung heroes of his story. They showed him what worked by identifying what didn't. Yes, make no mistake about it. Failure can be a great success.

Today, begin practicing some positive new math, failure plus learning equals success. Give yourself an enlightened lesson plan in which all experiences are valued for the unique education they bring. When viewed from this perspective, your time on Earth cannot help but add up to a resounding triumph.

VOICES

Bad times have a scientific value. These are occasions a good learner would not miss.

Ralph Waldo Emerson

Mistakes are the portals of discovery.

James Joyce

The greatest mistake in life is to be continually fearing you will make a mistake.

Elbert Hubbard

Man can not discover new oceans unless he has the courage to leave the shore.

Andre Gide

Learn to get in touch with the silence within yourself, and know that everything in life has purpose. There are no mistakes, no coincidences, all events are blessings given to us to learn from.

Elisabeth Kubler-Ross

If I had to live my life over again, I'd try to make more mistakes next time.

Nadine Star

Freedom is not worth having if it does not connote freedom to err. It passes my comprehension how human beings, be they ever so experienced and able, can delight in depriving other human beings of that precious right.

Mohandas K. Gandhi

18

WAR IS NEVER HOLY

Of all the ways human beings shoot themselves in the foot and make life more difficult, war has got to be the worst. It is so self-destructive that it makes one question what humanity is truly aiming for in this world. Even a fifth-grader knows that fighting is not the best way to solve problems. It just lengthens the time it takes to find common ground and lasting solutions. And, if the leaders of a species aren't as smart as fifth-graders, you certainly have to wonder about the long-term prospects for the species.

Humans killing humans is so perfectly counterproductive to the goals of human life it is beyond astounding that after thousands of years of being at each other's throats, we just can't seem to quit the habit. To be sure, the fear-based rationalizations our leaders dream up for war as they invoke the blessings of God on their behalf certainly play a big part.

These justifications get cloaked in all types of euphemisms, yet remain scary enough to keep war machines well funded and armies well populated. The Us-Versus-Them mentality is a depressingly easy headspace to create in our world. And, when you want to make a push become a shove, it is not too difficult to cook up an enemy to turn the population against.

To be fair, it must be stated that at our current level of evolution, there are unfortunately still times when it seems that force has to be met with force because it is the only language some combatants are swayed by. I don't think inviting Hitler to a spiritual seminar in the 1930s would have suddenly made him start belching rose petals and espousing the virtues of universal love.

(I suppose we could always just lie down in the face of aggressors and sacrifice our lives for peace, but it doesn't seem like the world is quite ready to go "all in" on that. Maybe check back in a few eons?)

However, Hitler did provide the world with a powerful learning opportunity. That is, should the world ever choose to be truly educated by it, which hasn't happened yet. Hitler demonstrated for all time what happens when the wrong mind takes over and starts running things. He also showed what happens when citizens of a nation don't question the status quo. Of course, most of us feel that this level of depravity could never befall us and, hopefully, we are right. But, in reality, our species supports war much more than most people know. That's probably because we are much more desensitized to its real toll than we care to admit.

For example, can someone living in a posh, peaceful suburb truly understand the effect of having a "smart bomb" land on your house, killing your entire family except for you? Can we really fathom what it would be like to have the light go out permanently in our lives for no other reason than someone got their coordinates wrong, or even worse, someone got some their coordinates right?

Or, if we were lucky enough to survive bombs falling on our heads and the mind-boggling use of chemical agents like white phosphorus – as reported by the BBC when it lands on the skin it often burns all the way down to the bone – can we really understand what it would be like to resume daily life in a toxic environment where our children are exposed to deadly levels of residual radiation from the depleted-uranium-tipped warheads used in weapons like "bunker busters" which are now considered conventional weapons?

According to a letter written to the United Nations by a group of concerned doctors, scientists and government officials in September 2009, Fallujah General Hospital in Iraq reportedly had 170 newborn babies. Of these, 24 percent died within the first seven days. 75 percent of the dead babies were classified as deformed, many severely. This can be compared with data from the month of August 2002, when there were 530 newborn babies, of whom six were dead within the first seven days, and only one birth defect was reported.

The letter stated that not only are doctors in Fallujah witnessing unprecedented numbers of birth defects, but also that premature births had increased considerably since 2003. Furthermore, it pointed out that, "a significant number of babies that do survive begin to develop severe disabilities at a later stage."

Further reporting by the BBC revealed the letter also stated that many young women in Fallujah had now become terrified of having babies because of the grotesque deformities they had witnessed. There was reportedly a case of a baby born with no head, another born with three heads and another born with a single eye in the middle of its forehead. In addition, the letter concluded that young children in the area were experiencing a significant rise in cancer.

The U.K. Guardian reported that abnormal clusters of infant tumors had also been documented in Fallujah and had been cited in Basra and Najaf as well, two other intense battle zones where modern munitions were heavily used. A group of Iraqi and British officials, including the former Iraqi minister for women's affairs, Dr Nawal Majeed a-Sammarai, and the British doctors David Halpin and Chris Burns-Cox, petitioned the UN General Assembly to ask for an independent committee to investigate the birth defects.

Can we honestly imagine what it would be like to have the first question after a young mother gives birth no longer be, "Is it a boy or girl?" but rather, "Is it deformed?" No, we can't, and this disconnect gives the world the cover it needs to grind on in its struggling state.

The real cumulative suffering in our world just seems to be too much for most of us to process or handle. So instead, we remain selectively de-linked from what many of our brothers and sisters across the globe suffer through on a regular basis. We get more involved with characters and storylines on fictional TV shows and reality shows than real life storylines in war-torn countries.

We also remain selectively amnesiac to what has happened in the past. We keep our blinders on so we can maintain some semblance of happiness and walk around with a smile on our face at least part of the time. And this is somewhat understandable. But we do so at a cost.

Everyone knows about the incomprehensible human toll of the big wars like World War I (16 million killed, 21 million wounded) and World War II (more than 60 million killed). But the reality is that our planet has been infested with war since humans first chose to kill each other.

That's when the cycle of attack and counter-attack first got started. It is estimated by some that in recorded history, humans have not been in a state of war somewhere across the Earth only 2 percent of the time. If you find that hard to believe, wrap your head around the estimated numbers of people who have been killed in "major" conflicts other than World War I and II in just the 20th century alone:

Congo Free State (1886-1908): 8,000,000

Mexican Revolution (1910-20): 1,000,000

Armenian Massacres (1915-23): 1,500,000

China, Warlord Era (1917-28): 800,000

China, Nationalist Era (1928-37): 3,100,000

Korean War (1950-53): 2,800,000

North Korea (1948 et seq.): It is estimated that the Communist regime of North Korea committed 1,663,000 democides between 1948 and 1987.

Rwanda and Burundi (1959-95): 1,350,000

Second Indochina War (1960-75): 3,500,000 (Cambodia, Laos and Vietnam)

Ethiopia (1962-92): 1,400,000

Nigeria (1966-70): 1,000,000

Bangladesh (1971): 1,250,000

Cambodia, Khmer Rouge (1975-1978): 1,650,000

Mozambique (1975-1992): 1,000,000

Afghanistan (1979-2001): 1,800,000

Iran-Iraq War (1980-88): 1,000,000

Sudan (1983 et seq.): 1,900,000

Kinshasa Congo (1998 et seq.): 3,800,000

Here are the estimated numbers of people killed from what are classified as "secondary" conflicts:

Philippines Insurgency (1899-1902): 220,000
Brazil (1900 et seq.): 500,000
Amazonia (1900-12): 250,000
Portuguese Colonies (1900-25): 325,000
French Colonies (1900-40): 200,000
Russo-Japanese War (1904-05): 130,000
Maji-Maji Revolt German East Africa (1905-07): 175,000
Libya (1911-31): 125,000
Balkan Wars (1912-13): 140,000
Greco-Turkish War (1919-1922): 250,000
Turkey (1925-28): 250,000
Spanish Civil War (1936-39) and Franco Regime (1939-75): 365,000 + 100,000
Abyssinian Conquest (1935-41): 400,000
Russo-Finnish War (1939-1940): 150,000
Greek Civil War (1943-49): 158,000
Yugoslavia, Tito's Regime (1944-80): 200,000
First Indochina War (1945-54): 400,000
Colombia (1946-58): 200,000
India (1947): 500,000
Romania (1948-89): 150,000
Burma/ Myanmar (1948 et seq.): 130,000
Algeria (1954-62): 537,000
Sudan (1955-72): 500,000
Guatemala (1960-1996): 200,000
Indonesia (1965-66): 400,000
Uganda, Idi Amin's regime (1972-79): 300,000
Vietnam, post-war Communist regime (1975 et seq.): 430,000
Angola (1975-2002): 550,000
East Timor, Conquest by Indonesia (1975-99): 200,000
Lebanon (1975-90): 150,000
Cambodian Civil War (1978-91): 225,000

Iraq, Saddam Hussein (1979-2003): 300,000
Uganda (1979-86): 300,000
Kurdistan (1980s, 1990s): 300,000
Liberia (1989-97): 150,000
Iraq (1990-Present): 350,000
Bosnia and Herzegovina (1992-95): 175,000
Somalia (1991 et seq.): 400,000
Zaire (Dem. Rep. Congo), Civil War (1997): 250,000

Here are the estimated numbers of people killed from what are classified as even smaller, "mid-range" conflicts:

Dutch East Indies, Aceh War (1873-1914): 70,000
Boxer Rebellion (1899-1901): 115,000
Anglo-Boer War (1899-1902): 75,000
Colombia (1899-1902): 100,000
Somalia, Mohammed Abdulla Hasan (1899-1920): 100,000
Russia (1900-17): 95,000
Herero War, German Southwest Africa (1904-07): 75,000
Russo-Polish War (1918-1920): 100,000
Morocco (1921-26): 68,000
Manchuria (1931-33): 60,000
Chaco War (1932-35): 100,000
Israel (1948 et seq.): 65,000
East Germany (1949-89): 100,000
Congo Crisis (1960-64): 100,000
Iraq (1960s): 100,000
Angola (1961-75): 80,000
Mozambique Anti-colonial war (1961-75): 63,500
North Yemen (1962-70): 100,000
Nicaragua (1972-91): 60,000
Philippines (1972-): 120,000
Colombia (1970s, 1980s, 90s): 45,000
El Salvador (1979-92): 75,000
Sierra Leone (1991-2002): 75,000

Algeria (1992-2002): 100,000
Eritrea-Ethiopia War (1998-2000): 70,000

There are many other conflicts that killed anywhere from 1,000 to 40,000 people, but they are too numerous to mention here. This list also doesn't take into account the financial cost of wars. Imagine how much brighter our world's future would be if we re-prioritized and put all the money we spend on war into creating shared interests and common ground between nations, cultures and religions and building a global economy that is based on peace, not war. Establishing Departments of Peace in governments across the globe certainly is the logical and long overdue first step.

Because anyway you look at it, this is a brawling planet. Especially when you consider that what our world classifies as merely "secondary" conflicts all wiped out the equivalent populations of nice-sized cities. If this constitutes our thinking, then no matter how well we dress our self-inflicted wounds, we remain one very injured patient.

To flip this around and put the amputated leg on the other foot, what if every time a country went to war, it automatically lost an entire city of people as price of admission? Like how about:

Lincoln, Nebraska; population - 251,624
Madison, Wisconsin; population - 231,916
Orlando, Florida; population - 230,519
Scottsdale, Arizona; population - 235,371
Buffalo, New York; population - 270,919
Greensboro, North Carolina; population - 250, 642
Fort Wayne, Indiana; population - 251,591
Reno, Nevada; population - 217,016
Laredo, Texas; population - 221,659
Norfolk, Virginia; population - 234,220
Jersey City, New Jersey; population - 241,114
St. Paul, Minnesota; population - 279,590

The populations of these cities are all in the rough ballpark of the estimated 250,000 people that perished in the civil war in Zaire in 1997. To put this loss of life in a different perspective, for a round number let's say the average high school contains 1,000 promising young adults.

This means the deaths in Zaire represent the combined hopes, dreams and potential of 250 high schools with 1,000 students each, all wiped out because of poor conflict resolution. What community would willingly offer up that type of sacrifice for war if it were the young adults in their high schools who would be erased?

In the war for a Congo Free State from 1886-1908, an estimated 8 million people died. (For comparison, there were an estimated 8,337,000 people living in New York City in 2012.) We would have to start pillaging maternity wards, nursery schools, elementary schools, junior high schools, senior high schools, colleges, graduate schools, the work force and retirement homes to accommodate the Grim Reaper on that one. Yet, when we don't see the whole world as our community, we allow these things to take place. A world like this is no earthly paradise. It's an insane asylum.

Considering the profound suffering war brings to the world, there must be something awfully powerful at work to keep us fighting. And there are certainly many theories bandied about to try to explain why it is we fight.

According to one provocative theory, genes use human life as a way to perfect themselves. War and violence cull the herd and perpetuate stronger genes. Humans, especially men, because they are the heroes usually sent off to war – an estimated 80% of Soviet males born in 1923 didn't survive World War II – are just the clay with which genes perfect their creations.

This theory contends that the genes passed on are the ones which serve the gene's own implicit interests, which are to continue being replicated, and not necessarily those of the host organism. Based on this analysis, our lives only matter as much as they further our genes' goals. How's that for a perky interpretation of the meaning of life?

If blaming our genes doesn't suffice, there is always money and greed. The obscenely lucrative defense industry is a big supplier of jobs and attracts some of our finest minds to its programs. It is a government-mandated display of the Us-Versus-Them mentality and it means big business to keep this culture of fear going. National economies and enormous amounts of wealth depend on it.

But how critical is our level of creature comfort and earning power when it means others have to be killed or maimed for life so we can make enough money off war-related industries to afford a few extra bedrooms and a three-car garage? Living in a pup tent seems preferable to that.

Of course, we can also always blame God. There is no greater creator of conflict on Earth than the desire to convert lesser souls to higher religions. It doesn't matter which of the major religions you choose, they have pretty much all done it. They all fall prey to the curious ego belief that to get closer to God and spread God's word, you must kill God's misguided creations, those unfortunate non-believers or wrongdoers. Talk about a bad marketing plan.

Or, if blaming God seems unwise, especially since so many have him pegged as the social director for our afterlife, we could always blame good old "manifest destiny." In the modern world, this mother of all rationalizations has now morphed into the mission to promote capitalism throughout the world or, if that's not your thing, communism or socialism or some form of theocracy or fill in the blank_____. Even if it means killing people to give them a better life.

It is certainly understandable that countries want to share what they believe to be the benefits of their way of life with other countries. These kinds of interchanges contribute to the richness of our world and help us learn about societies that are remote from us.

But this exchange is always more effectively accomplished through the peaceful sharing of mind, rather than force of will or body. If it requires physical invasions and violence to make our point, the point simply needs to be rethought. The worst thing any generation can bequeath to the next generation, besides a ruined environment, is a lower threshold for going to war.

Yet regrettably, in our world there still seem to be plenty of reasons to jump into a fight. And so the drumbeat of war pounds on and our tired, weary world drags itself through conflict after bloody conflict. One of my biggest hopes is that future generations will look back at these times as the dark ages. That at least would mean we had evolved beyond these self-defeating ways of thinking.

So what do we do about the pugnacious people of "Planet Pugilism" and our much glorified fighting spirit? Where does all this killing come from anyway? In the mind, of course. How do you get it to stop? In the mind. And the first thing to do is to stop blaming others for wars. Blame is just a different kind of war. Instead, let's take responsibility for war in the one place we can, our mind.

Because we're not really anti-war if we are still fighting with people in our minds.

We're not really anti-war if we think some people deserve to be told off and administered a verbal thrashing rather than be given a helping hand up.

We're not really anti-war if we want to crush our business competitors by any means possible.

We're not really anti-war if we like to ridicule and attack other people's supposed shortcomings.

We're not really anti-war if we relish when celebrities, athletes or politicians fall from grace.

We're not really anti-war if we enjoy creating or watching gratuitously violent movies and television shows in which people get killed solely for the sake of entertainment and the perceived value of human life is reduced to zero. Imagine if an advanced race of nonviolent beings came to Earth and saw us entertaining ourselves in this fashion. I doubt our planet would ever make their list of preferred vacation destinations.

We're not really anti-war if for us to gain, everybody else has to lose.

We're not really anti-war if an eye-for-an-eye seems like perfect justice. As Gandhi wisely pointed out, an eye-for-an-eye and the whole world goes blind.

We're not really anti-war if we want to strangle the person on the other side of the political or religious spectrum.

And we're most definitely not really anti-war if we are masters at holding grievances. As the timeless spiritual teaching states, holding a grievance is like injecting yourself with poison and thinking it will kill your enemy.

In fact, it is wise not to be "anti" anything. It's negative energy no matter how you couch it. Mother Theresa expressed this perfectly when she was asked to take part in an anti-war demonstration. She declined, but said she would be happy to march for peace. She knew anti-war demonstrations could be some of the most hawkish gatherings of all.

If war does break your heart though, like it does to so many, the greatest elixir in our troubled world is to make our mind a place where war doesn't exist. We need to transform our mind into a sacred space where only peace reigns. Because what is happening in our mind is on a collective basis, often what is happening in our world. It's all connected.

Considering this, we are far too free and easy with our anger. We throw it around like it's just harmless dust that disappears the second our rage passes. Furthermore, we believe it is our righteous privilege to do so. But, by standing up for our right to fight, we are propping up a world where war becomes the ultimate extension of this. The cycle of attack and counterattack thus continues on forever.

Thankfully though there is a way to offer up the kind of beauty needed in a quarrelsome world like ours to tame the savage beast. Forget about the Hope Diamond. Our mind is the most precious gem in the universe, and keeping it peaceful and forgiving is the most healing gift we can give the world.

Admittedly, maintaining internal peace requires a lot of effort. If it were natural to us, wars would not be. As humans, we are at a bit of a disadvantage because of how our brains are wired. Sensory input goes to the emotional part of our brains before the higher thinking part of our brains. This accounts for crimes of passion and people flying off the handle before they have time to think about what they are doing.

By becoming aware of this, we put ourselves back in control. This awareness must then be strengthened until it becomes second nature to us before we act to think about the greatest good instead of the greatest revenge. It must always be remembered that reacting emotionally is simply a muscle. The way to weaken it is to not use it. The way to not use it is to cultivate awareness.

We are all familiar with controlled burns that help the Forest Service manage fire conditions. Similarly, training ourselves to remain rational at all times helps us control our internal fire conditions. When we do this, we will find ourselves less prone to emotional brushfires and more invested in keeping the peace.

The ultimate payoff from this kind of investment is that war automatically makes less sense. We can try and justify war all we want, and many do. But in the end, all we are arguing for is the right to live in a violent world deeply scarred by the low roads we choose that cut a path of destruction across the human heart.

Of course, by cultivating peace in our mind it doesn't mean that all the world's holy wars – and all wars are holy to the leaders who wage them – will suddenly reach a truce. But at least the ones in our mind will. And that is a huge start.

Because it's the ones who live peacefully and become peace who are the most effective promoters of peace in the world. And they do it just by being the peaceful, forgiving, compassionate folks they are. So it's a win-win no matter how you look at it. To me, that's a goal worth shooting for.

Voices

When the power of love overcomes the love of power the world will know peace.

Jimi Hendrix

Peace cannot be kept by force. It can only be achieved by understanding.

Albert Einstein

For the great Gaels of Ireland, are the men that God made mad, for all their wars are merry and all their songs are sad.

G.K. Chesterton

I dream of giving birth to a child who will ask, 'Mother, what was war?

Eve Merriam

If a man gives up a fight when he is wrong, a house will be built for him in Paradise. But if a man gives up a fight even when he is in the right, a house will be built for him on the loftiest realm of Paradise.

Muhammad

Have we not come to such an impasse in the modern world that we must love our enemies – or else? The chain reaction of evil – hate begetting hate, wars producing more wars – must be broken, or else we shall be plunged into the dark abyss of annihilation.

Martin Luther King

Fighting for peace is like screwing for virginity.

George Carlin

19

FORGIVENESS IS THE WORLD'S MOST ADVANCED TECHNOLOGY

Sometimes our world seems to be on a cosmic hamster wheel, chugging and chugging and chugging, but getting nowhere. The second one problem is fixed, another one pops right up to replace it. Need to get around quicker? Retire the horse and invent the automobile. Now we have gridlock, oil spills, air pollution and millions of miles of roads to maintain.

Want to enhance our ability to communicate? Invent the internet. Now we have cyber attacks, a proliferation of misinformation, a loss of corporate productivity and questionable content viewed by minors.

Want to cure disease? Bombard the populace with miraculous medicine. Now we have rampant drug dependency, over-taxed livers and inhumanly high insurance rates. Plus, it is now estimated by some that 30 percent of all medical problems are caused by the side effects from medicines and medical treatments.

Want to protect your citizens from the barbarians at the gate? Invent nuclear weapons. Now we have a nuclear arms race and more money spent on weapons than education.

What to do about this vexing world of ours and the problem of our multiplying problems? Traditional advanced technologies have certainly done enormous good in the world and have solved many previously unsolvable problems. But unfortunately, they can't fix everything in an imperfect world like ours.

Nano-technology, robotics, artificial intelligence, systems analysis, nuclear medicine, genetics, etc., we won't find all the answers we are looking for there. Those are inventions of the mind designed to fix problems in the world, a world that loves to create endless new challenges for itself, even as old challenges are overcome.

To pick up the slack, what we also need is an invention of the mind to fix problems in the mind. The problems I am referring to are judgment and attachment. The miraculous invention that cures them is forgiveness.

You want to fix all the world's problems in one fell swoop? There is no cure-all in the entire world like forgiving the world and the people in it for their imperfections. Plus, forgiveness comes with no negative side effects and a vast array of side benefits. You don't need wisdom teachers from centuries ago to tell you the advantages of forgiveness. You can experience them for yourself.

Want to help cure disease? Forgiveness removes bitterness that feeds disease.

Want to live longer and age more slowly? Forgiveness breeds a positive outlook, which boosts immunity and slows the aging process.

Want to add more comfort to your life? Forgiveness removes thorns from your side, enabling you to live and breathe easier.

Want to lessen the problem of our over-crowded highways and ever-lengthening commutes? Forgiveness helps cure road rage.

Want to improve international relations? Forgiveness tears down walls and brings countries together, even ancient enemies.

Want to lessen armed conflict? No war has ever been fought over forgiveness.

Want a government that works for the people? Forgiveness promotes bipartisanship.

Want to get great things accomplished in this lifetime? Forgiveness grows your team, removes emotional roadblocks and maximizes your capabilities.

Want to have stronger muscles and feel more alive? During muscle-strength testing, people get stronger and have greater stamina when thinking loving, forgiving thoughts rather than negative ones.

Want to get inspired? Forgiveness removes the dead weight from your psyche, liberating your mind to ascend to higher states.

Want to feel more love in your life? When you forgive, love can't help but blossom.

Want to stop fearing for your safety? Forgiveness means you don't attack others so you don't have to spend your time worrying about being attacked in return.

Want to sleep better? When you have no enemies, sleep is more restful and dreams are more peaceful.

Want to overcome social anxiety? When you look for the good in people instead of the bad, the world you live in becomes more inviting.

Want to have better memories? Forgive your past.

Want to have a brighter future? Forgive your past.

Want to enjoy nature more? Nothing kills a great hike in the woods like an angry mind.

Want to have more charisma? Nothing is more attractive than someone who says only positive things about others.

Want to suffer less-bitter breakups? Forgive your ex-lovers and sometimes they remain in your life as friends, sometimes even best friends. Imagine that.

Want to feel a deep peace that cannot be disturbed? When you forgive, peace is what you become.

Obviously, forgiving others is not always easy to do. Despite how miserable they tend to makes us, grudges and grievances are something we often have a very hard time letting go of. There are some who would rather empty their bank accounts than let go of a grudge. They will pay therapists good money week after week to retell stories of their mistreatment at the hands of others.

There are others who would rather die than let go of a grudge. The famous feud between the Hatfields and McCoys is a perfect example of this. Regrettably, quarrels are so commonplace in our world they are no longer even all that noteworthy.

Everyone knows of people who are always in attack mode and who spend their lives condemning others. In their fear, they believe that attack keeps them safe and rights the perceived wrongs in the world. In actuality though, condemnation never brings safety or peace. It only brings a conflict-ridden mind and leaves shattered relationships in its wake. Thankfully, a little bit of true forgiveness changes all of that.

True forgiveness is grounded in the classic spiritual idea that states we are the projector of the dream we call our life, rather than the figure in the dream. If this is true then everything we are experiencing, we are doing to ourselves. Therefore, it follows that we should forgive our brothers and sisters for what they did not do to us because it is all our own creation.

The beauty to this approach is that it grants forgiveness to everybody equally and unconditionally. It also takes the whole messy question of guilt and sin completely out of the picture. Plus, it heals the mind of the forgiver because forgiveness is ultimately a gift we give ourselves.

For some people, this notion might seem a bit too radical. To others it may sound like an over-simplification. But any mental framework that helps us forgive is worth exploring because forgiveness is the key to happiness. We could have everything else in the world we want, but if we can't forgive, happiness will be beyond our reach.

And if you're the type that feels some people don't deserve forgiveness no matter what, regardless if life is a dream or not, then it might help to take a deeper look at what is really happening at the core of our human interaction.

No matter how many different ways we get approached by people, there is always only one of two things that is ever really happening. As *A Course in Miracles* teaches, people are either expressing love or they are crying out for love.

If they are expressing love, the perfect response is to be loving. If they are crying out for love by lashing out and attacking others, the perfect response is to be loving. So the perfect response every time, in every circumstance, is to be loving. And when you're loving, forgiveness comes naturally. Life is so much easier this way.

So many thanks go to whatever distant ancestor first forgave. Maybe it was an enlightened primate who forgave his mate for stealing his healthy, unprocessed raw meal. Or, maybe it was a single-cell organism that forgave its cell lover for combining with another cell.

Whoever came up with forgiveness though, gave us the ability to regain control of our world by not letting the world take total control of our mind. What other "technologies" can do that? There are none. This makes forgiveness the world's greatest technology. Try it out today and see what the most advanced thinking on the planet can do for you. It doesn't even require instructions.

VOICES

To forgive is to set a prisoner free and discover that the prisoner was you.

Lewis B. Smedes

If you want to make peace with your enemy, you have to work with your enemy. Then he becomes your partner.

Nelson Mandela

There is no love without forgiveness. And there is no forgiveness without love.

Bryant H. McGill

Without forgiveness, there is no future.

Desmond Tutu

Forgiveness means giving up all hopes for a better past.

Jerry Jampolsky and Diane Cirincione

Since nothing we intend is ever faultless, and nothing we attempt ever without error, and nothing we achieve without some measure of finitude and fallibility we call humanness, we are saved by forgiveness.

David Augsnurger

Forgiveness is the fragrance that the violet sheds on the heel that has crushed it.

Mark Twain

20

LAUGHTER IS THE SOUND OF GOOD HEALTH

On my deathbed I want to get the giggles.

I want to laugh so hard that I crack up 'till I croak. If fate grants me a pause before the final unveiling, I want to fill it with guffaws so deep that I suck all the oxygen out of the room and replace it with laughing gas. That would be a strong way to transition. It would stamp your life as time well spent because you had used it to master your own mind.

If you were of high enough spirit that you could giggle at your body's demise, the entire universe would have to metaphorically bow down to your will. By choosing your state of mind to be independent from circumstance, you would render circumstance irrelevant. You would be dictating terms to life, rather than depending on its limited mercy for your happiness.

Developing an indestructible sense of humor is something everyone should do in this world, especially considering life is so often absurd. After all, any realm in which the hapless creatures have to eat each other to stay alive needs some serious comic relief. Any realm that has more weapons in it than folks who practice forgiveness should come with an endless supply of cackles, snickers and yuk yuks.

Any realm where a big space rock could end life on Earth in an instant requires some prodigious belly-laughing skills. Any realm that gives birth to incomprehensible moments in history like these demands some serious chuckle muscles otherwise we might all lose our minds or die of broken hearts:

430 BC. Empedocles, pre-Socratic philosopher, jumped into an active volcano (Mt. Etna) to convince his contemporaries that he had been taken in and was protected by the gods of Olympus.

456 BC. Aeschylus is said to have been killed when an eagle dropped a tortoise out of the sky onto his head, which it had mistaken for a rock.

260. Roman Emperor Valerian, after being defeated in battle and captured by the Persians, was supposedly used as a footstool by King Shapur before being skinned alive.

1673. Molière, the French actor and playwright, died after being seized by a violent coughing fit while playing the title role in his play, *Le Malade Imaginaire.* (*The Hypochondriac*).

1814. In "The London Beer Flood", nine people were killed when 323,000 gallons of beer in the Meux and Company Brewery burst out of their vats and gushed into the streets. Many of those who didn't drown were seen scooping up the free brew and drinking it with unrestrained glee. The disaster/party was eventually ruled an act of God by the judge and jury, leaving no one responsible.

Yes, this is an often-absurd realm and being tickled to death by it all is a healthy reaction to the inscrutability of human existence. In a sense, it is no reaction at all. You are not taking the bait and getting pulled into the seriousness of the world. You are exercising detachment, remaining in the bleachers and taking in the entertainment.

You are in your right mind and so, even at the show's end, you can giggle at the body's demise because deep down you know it is not you. You're just there observing. And ironically, by not taking the world and your life too seriously, you actually give the world and your life your best effort. You don't burn precious life energy on senseless melodrama.

Seriousness just insures everything stays serious. So at some point you must break through the seriousness to the humor. It is your reward for enduring life's joyless passages like root canals, tax time, small talk and jury duty and nothing makes the soul smile deeper than laughter. A good gut-buster almost feels divine, like you are in cahoots with the supreme intelligence of the universe in an inside cosmic joke.

In moments of hysterical laughter, you can see clearly that none of it really matters. How could it if you are laughing that hard? And if nothing matters, that means you are free to view life as a comedy and then enjoy the heck out of playing your part. In fact, when I think about exiting this realm, one of the things I would miss most is cracking up. Laughing hysterically is a sign of sanity. It tells you so much about a person's true well-being, which is the well-being of their mind.

I remember a story a good buddy of mine related to me in college about a friend of his who was told that there was a car on fire on campus. His friend was curious to check it out and so he trotted off in the direction of the fire engines. When he got there, he realized the shiny new car on fire was his. Did he freak out, curse fate and start looking for someone to blame?

No.

He got the giggles.

Then he asked a fireman if he had a marshmallow. Then they both got the giggles. Some people would call that crazy. I call that the peak of sanity.

The mother of another friend of mine was doing poorly and was in the intensive care unit at a hospital. His mother had one collapsed lung and had fluid in her other lung. She had lost a lot of weight, and her failing body was threatening to end the show at any moment. She was too weak to walk so as a last-ditch effort, the staff had placed her on a bed that vibrated in an effort to clear some of the fluid from her lung.

Members of the family were gathered around. This was the moment my friend had rehearsed in his mind and he recognized it as the final vigil. The mood in the room was very somber. Suddenly the emotion of the moment overcame my friend and his family. Seeing their bedraggled matriarch being jiggled to death on her vibrating deathbed was just too much for them to handle. So they did the only thing they could do. They got the giggles.

When their deathly-ill mother peered across the room and saw her husband and children giggling at her, she did the only thing she could do. She got the giggles too. When some of the staff came in the room to see what was going on – a giggle fest is not a nor-mal occurrence in an intensive care unit – they did the only thing they could do. They also got the giggles. Now the whole room was giggling uncontrollably, orchestrated by my friend's mother on her jiggling, giggling deathbed.

They all proceeded to enjoy an uproarious moment together and, amazingly enough, soon after, my friend's mother reversed direction, got stronger and checked out of the hospital. As of this writing she is doing much better.

For years people have reported recovering from serious illness by undergoing a form of laugh therapy. In this enlightened medical treatment, they are sequestered in a room where they watch hour after hour of comedies. The laughter in their soul heals the illness in their body and some make full recoveries.

If laugher can do this for deathly-ill folks, think about what it can do for healthy people. And luckily, you don't even need a stack of comedy DVDs to get you going. Just review your own life! Just think of all the times absurdity has ruled the moment. There is so much to giggle at. Allow me to get us started.

I remember the time I woke up early to do some writing, burn-ing with inspiration. I lived alone at the time and after I had stripped down to take a shower, suddenly something crossed my mind that had to be written at that very moment. You think the call of a soothing hot shower is powerful? It's nothing compared to the moment when a writer feels he actually might have something worthwhile to say.

So instead of hopping in the shower, I walked naked out to my desk in the living room. There was simply no time to dress when inspiration was calling that loudly, and besides, it was a warm sum-mer morning anyway.

I quickly sat down at my computer and started pounding the keys in the buff. As I was writing, I suddenly realized I had forgotten to return an important phone call from the night before. I picked up the phone and dialed and, to my frustration, the call wouldn't connect. I tried a few more times and still it wouldn't connect. It would only ring once and then it was just dead air.

I hung up the phone and debated what to do. I soon realized I better call for some technical assistance and see what was happening. I dialed the three-digit number for repair, but then impulsively decided I wasn't ready to get into an inspiration-killing conversation with the humorless folks at the phone company.

So I quickly hung up and dove back into my writing. A few minutes later, as I was surfing the waves of inspiration in my mind, I heard a noise outside my front door. At the time, I was living in a security-monitored building so people never just appeared at my door. They had to be buzzed in from outside.

(Too bad we can't utilize a similar arrangement for fearful thoughts that appear at the door of our mind.

"Who's there?"

"The thought of failure."

"Sorry, the buzzer is broken.")

I dove back into my work and after about a minute I heard another noise outside my door. Curious to find out what it was, I walked up to the front door naked and looked through the tiny peephole. Through the distorting wide-angle lens of the peephole, I saw a group of people dressed in black on the other side of my door.

As I pulled back and began to ponder their identity and purpose, suddenly my locked front door opened and the end of a shiny gun slid through the opening. With the firearm came the most serious multiple-choice question of my life, fight or flight? Having nowhere to run or any clothes on to run in, I chose fight. I threw my body against the door and tried to shut it with all my might, but was overwhelmed by the force pushing back on the other side.

I was thrown back from the door and, as it flew open, I was bull-rushed by a group of highly motivated protectors of the peace. As the first police officer pushed toward me, the muzzle of his firearm made icy contact with my throat. In this quick motion, my very existence was called into question and, even worse, my unfinished writing project.

As my heartbeat went double-time and jumped into my throat, my body went on autopilot. In my mortal fear, my body came up with the one thing it apparently thought might save my butt. It involuntarily shot a perfectly arching stream of bright yellow pee into the air.

At that moment, it was as if someone had hit the slow motion button on the movie projector of my life. The dutiful officer and I, suddenly directed by fate to join in a surreal, half naked, Greco-Roman slow dance, watched together as the stream of liquid fear scored a direct hit on his shiny black boot. The last thing I remember him saying was, "Hey, that's my foot!" Then he and the rest of the officers threw me on the floor face down and handcuffed my wrists behind my back.

As I lay there bare-butt naked, pressed down into my remarkably itchy carpet wearing only my embarrassment, I realized that two of the officers were ladies and were actually quite attractive. (I confess. For some people, there is never a bad time to admire the incredible beauty of the female form.) At that point, I decided to surrender in my mind and see where the moment would take me. My body had surrendered already.

Their commanding officer asked me if there was anyone else in the apartment as the others looked around and quickly secured the premises. After I told him I lived alone, he then informed me that someone had called 911 and then hung up, and they took that as a call for help.

It was then that I realized that instead of dialing 611 for repair, I must have dialed 911 by mistake. This gave them the giggles, but I wasn't quite ready to join them seeing as I was still lying naked by their feet with my inglorious white moon illuminating the room.

Eventually it all got sorted out and they stood me up, uncuffed me and told me to be more careful how I dialed the phone. As I was lying at their feet, I had been searching for the moral of the story and there it was: "Be careful how you dial the phone."

Then they were gone, leaving me standing naked in my apartment once again, but now the proud owner of a pride-smashing bad moment and the inspiration for years of guffaws as the story was retold. Then I sat down on the floor and laughed hysterically until my stomach ached. Working on my non-existent six-pack abs never felt so good.

Classic moments like these now go into my "cringer file", which is a compilation of all the incredibly embarrassing moments I've had in my life. I like to review the file mentally from time to time when I need a good laugh. It helps me not take life or myself too seriously, and keeps my mind in a decompressed state.

The more often I laugh, the better off I know I am so I spend a lot of time with my cringer file. To be honest, I don't know where I'd be without it.

As I have gotten older I have come to believe that getting the giggles is actually serious business and is the one virus everyone should hope to catch in this lifetime. With any luck, it will be the one virus for which the world never finds a cure.

VOICES

Laughter is the sun that drives winter from the human face.

Victor Hugo

What soap is to the body, laughter is to the soul.

Yiddish Proverb

Laughter is the closest distance between two people.

Victor Borge

The most wasted of all days is one without laughter.

EE Cummings

The ultimate test of whether you possess a sense of humor is your reaction when someone tells you you don't.

Frank Tyger

21

KIND SPEECH ALWAYS COMPLIMENTS THE SPEAKER

For being so negative, negativity sure is popular in our world. It has become prevalent in so many different parts of society that you have to wonder who left the door to our realm open so it could wander in. Because now it's like the unruly guest at the dinner party who no one can seem to take their eyes off of.

On the internet, negative headlines achieve higher click-through rates than positive headlines. Radio and TV talk shows that do a lot of attacking often enjoy rabid followings, having forgotten along the way to high ratings that, just because something gains an audience in our world, doesn't mean it deserves an audience. Politicians have made the unfortunate discovery that negative ads and inflammatory rhetoric not only work, but they can change the course of history through their effect on elections:

A member of the British parliament to Benjamin Disraeli: "Sir, you will either die on the gallows, or of some unspeakable disease."

"That depends, Sir," said Disraeli, "on whether I embrace your policies or your mistress."

Gossip magazines do a brisk, negative business showering the public with the supposed dirty laundry of celebrity personal lives, overlooking the fact that you don't have to be famous to have dirty laundry, just human. Networks and movie studios dedicate large chunks of their production budgets to creating negative subject matter, especially crime and murder storylines. They know viewers will tune in as long as the stuff they pump out stays at a certain low vibration. It is quite a trick actually because if these same criminals came in through the viewer's window instead of through their television screen, they would immediately call the police.

Yes, without a doubt, one of the most inauspicious developments for the modern world was when content creators realized they could guarantee an audience when they catered to the part of the brain that creates traffic backups just to get a good view of an accident scene. In the end though, it all seems like a terribly odd way to spend one's time, so focused on the negative. For labors like these, we were given the miracle of life?

Flo: "I've never been so insulted in all my life!"

Groucho: "Well, it's early yet."

For anyone looking in from the outside, all this self-inflicted negativity would seem to scream that the human experiment cannot yet be called a positive success. An objective observer would have to conclude that we are in a clumsy growing stage at best, with a lot of refining yet to be done. And what makes this rampant negativity even more troublesome is that, over time, it lowers society's collective vibration to the point where negativity no longer even offends. It actually feels normal. In this diminished spiritual state, we then find other negative aspects of life, like unkind speech, all that more acceptable.

"If you were my husband, I'd give you poison."
Lady Astor

"If you were my wife, I'd drink it."
Winston Churchill

Amidst all the great pleasures of being alive, there are obviously also a lot of unsavory things that occur. In fact, there are enough bad times that happen all on their own that you would think folks would do anything to avoid creating more. How many times do you have to step on a rusty nail before you figure out it is not conducive to a happy journey?

> "I didn't attend the funeral, but I sent a
> nice letter saying I approved of it."
> Mark Twain

That is why it is so curious that unkind speech gets such a free pass. After all, it's just a guarantee of another bad time. Especially considering that no matter how witty and on target the unkind speech seems, it is always in the end a form of self-attack. It is simply impossible to be a processor of that type of energy and not be brought down by it. And yet, through such joyless endeavors as criticism, gossip, fault-finding, ridicule, condemnation, blame and the like, human beings have developed a huge tool set for breaking each other down and creating more negativity for the world to slog through.

> "I liked your opera. I think I will set it to music."
> Ludwig van Beethoven

The human mind is essentially a production facility that manufactures moments. When we become a processor of anything other than kindness, we essentially become a manufacturer of bad moments. All the gifts we've been given to enjoy an enlightened and evolutionary life are thus put to work at a toxic facility whose end product lowers the energy of everyone it touches, beginning first and foremost with the owner of the facility.

> "I have never killed a man, but I have read
> many obituaries with great pleasure."
> Clarence Darrow

Our ancestors struggled through great physical deprivations and genetic limitations to give our higher mind time to develop. In one sense, you could say they suffered to give us a choice later on in how we treat each other. With every famine our predecessors endured, every time they were literally eaten alive by predators, every brutal short life endured where 30-years-old was considered senior citizenship, our faithful forebearers inched human evolution along so future generations could enjoy more positive existences.

Not only do we live longer than ever before, we also have the free time to cultivate and embrace the higher instincts that lead to more compassionate living. To disregard all the struggle that made this luxury possible is like taking a Ferrari out for a test drive and immediately steering it over a cliff.

"His mind was like a soup dish, wide and shallow; it could hold a small amount of nearly anything, but the slightest jarring spilled the soup into somebody's lap."
Irving Stone writing about William Jennings Bryan

We have been given the keys to a wonderfully promising human experiment and our work in the present will determine what shape this experiment is in when it is handed off to future generations. Through our efforts, will the human race become more noble? Will it instinctively do the kind thing and lift up all that it comes in contact with?

"I've just learned about his illness. Let's hope it's nothing trivial."
Irvin S. Cobb

With so much hanging in the balance, it becomes a categorical imperative that we do everything in our power to turn ourselves into kindness production facilities. In a lot of ways, it is our most important work. And the great thing is, when we choose this as one of our occupations in life, we get to look good doing our job.

Unfortunately though, looking at the current state of affairs in the world, the outlook for a kind future remains cloudy at best.

Attacking others and saying something negative about someone seems to be one of humanity's juiciest, guilty pleasures. The rapid drop in elevation from the higher mind to the lower mind remains one of the most popular thrill rides in the amusement park of human consciousness.

> "I worship the quicksand he walks in."
> Art Buchwald

That we do this is somewhat understandable, considering we still have such a ravenous animal brain that needs to divide and conquer in any way possible. Homo Sapiens currently inhabiting Earth share the unenviable task of carrying a lower brain and a higher brain through this period of our evolution. Over the millennia, the lower brain has certainly become less weighty and dominant. But it is still there, and every time we drop down to it we take a trip back in evolution to a more brutish period in our history.

> "Have reserved two tickets for opening night.
> Come and bring a friend if you have one."
> George Bernard Shaw to Winston Churchill

> "Impossible to come to first night. Will come
> to second night if you have one."
> Winston Churchill to George Bernard Shaw

What's worse, every time we flex our animal/ego brain, we make it stronger, even though it is the one muscle that we should avoid exercising at all costs. Being strong at unkindness, otherwise known as being cruel, is an inelegant vestige leftover from a different era when a hardened heart was more crucial to our survival. But this hard shell must now be shed if humans are ever going to breakthrough to their full potential as spiritually enlightened beings.

"Wagner has beautiful moments, but awful quarter hours."
Gioacchino Rossini on Richard Wagner

"After Rossini dies, who will there be to promote his music?"
Richard Wagner on Gioacchino Rossini

Currently there are large portions of the human population that believe savaging people who "deserve it" constitutes a victory in this world and is a reasonable use of our mental faculties. When children do this on the playground though, we instinctively tell them that it is not nice because we would never want them to grow up thinking this is acceptable behavior. What kind of world would that lead to? Well, just look around because you are living in it.

Nowadays, even highly educated adults frequently say more scathing things about each other than children are even capable of thinking, and this is often considered perfectly acceptable behavior, especially if it gets us elected. Some people just need to be told off and you have to call a spade a spade, right? All is fair in love and war, right?

Wrong.

We win at nothing in life when we make someone else look bad in the process. Moments like that are just ego-inebriated stumbles off the path to enlightenment. Even if we win the verbal battle because we have pulled out the bigger artillery and have decimated our opponent, we haven't won anything of lasting value. We are merely preaching to the negative choir. Thoughtful folks are just not going to respond favorably to thoughtless attacks. Opposing positions just get hardened, bridges burned and everyone comes out looking bad in the process.

"Listening to the Fifth Symphony of Ralph Vaughan Williams is like staring at a cow for 45 minutes."
Aaron Copland

To get beyond these stumbling blocks on our journey to higher consciousness, it is helpful to remember that love does not attack or condemn. If we find ourselves doing either, we can safely assume our departure point was not love or strength, but fear. As *A Course in Miracles* teaches, love derives its strength from the fact that it is undivided. Only through division is attack even possible.

When the idea of attack has entered our mind, we must have perceived ourselves as weakened or divided in some sense. Maybe it was an attack we believe someone else did to us. Or maybe it was a self-inflicted attack. Or maybe it was just something in the world that threatened our self-esteem. But the way we often attempt to equalize the situation is by finding something to attack in return. This is why recognizing that we are love and, therefore, undivided and invulnerable to attack, is the key to regaining our peace. When attack has no effect, there is no longer any need to attack in return.

> "Poor Faulkner. Does he really think big emotions come from big words?"
> Ernest Hemingway

> "Hemingway has never been known to use a word that might send a reader to the dictionary."
> William Faulkner

But why even go through the insane dance of attack and counterattack in the first place, when there is a much easier way to achieve what we want in life, and to do it in style? You want to look good? You don't need snazzy clothes, great hair, witty comebacks or a wonderful physique. You don't have to attend the finest prep schools or be born into royalty. Just be kind.

Kind speech warms cold hearts and creates a loving space for everyone to come together and prosper. It builds bridges and creates loyalty and appreciation. When you are gentle, a kindly world will stretch out before you full of kind helpers who will assist you on your journey.

Obstructions will disappear, frustrations will minimize and your whole life will run more smoothly. The world itself will become a more loving place as its higher angels are called forth in everyone you shower with kindness. At the end of your life, regrets will be at a minimum because you will have put your best foot forward at all times.

The whole world just looks better when under the direction of kindness. And not just the human world. Think about a mama alligator that curbs her ravenous appetite and places her helpless hatchlings in her mouth to tenderly relocate them from the nest to the water. Suddenly, that gruesome grill becomes a safety den for its young and the mama gator looks actually lovable in the process.

Well, the same goes for humans. We may be dressed to the nines and be able to walk down the street like a moving piece of priceless, human art, but the second we say an unkind word, it's like dressing a pig in silk robes. We may be a highly educated member of Mensa, but the second we say something unkind, we look purely elementary. We may have the most beautiful features in the world, but say something unkind and we are instantly butt ugly.

"That's not writing; That's typing."
Truman Capote on Jack Kerouac

On the other hand, do you want to look great? Then make someone else look great. You want to pay yourself the ultimate compliment? Pay someone else the ultimate compliment. Be kind and you can surrender all outcomes and just enjoy watching life unfold. Everywhere you go doors will unlock and hearts will open. You will be bringing the sunshine with you, so you better expect a lot of warm welcomes. All you have to do is just be kind and you have predisposed reality to be kind in return. You will have done the kindest thing possible for yourself.

Besides, everybody needs love, without exception. There has never been a soul who walked the planet who didn't, and there never will be. And, before we all start pulling out our lists of those "special" folks in our lives we feel don't deserve love, I would like to share a healing perspective a kind person once shared with me:

It's the ones we find hardest to love in life
that need our love the most.

Once this simple truth is understood and embraced, the whole world opens up. Everywhere we look we will find another reason to be a processor of love and kindness. What could be more gratifying than that? Now we will have an instantaneous way to make magic out of every single interaction. Just be kind. Soon we will realize it doesn't even matter what we get back in return.

Every conversation will became an opportunity to deeply connect with someone, no matter what state they approach us in. By offering everyone a hand up verbally, transcendence will become a way of life rather than the rarest of occurrences. We will give everyone we meet a chance to be at his or her best in our presence. By simply remaining kind, we will become that most helpful of beings...a true healer. And, when we heal others, we cannot help but be healed ourselves.

Today pay yourself the perfect compliment and be kind to everyone you meet. Be a welcoming, safe port in the negative verbal storms that often ravage our planet. See everyone as yourself and speak to them as lovingly as you want to be spoken to. Once you have mastered this, you will have become rooted in your higher mind. Once you have become rooted in your higher mind, you will have mastered the world beyond your mind. And what a kind, beautiful world it will be.

"Even God is fond of a good joke."
Aristotle

VOICES

This is my simple religion. There is no need for temples: no need for complicated philosophy. Our own brain, our own heart is our temple: the philosophy is kindness.

Dalai Lama

If we could read the secret history of our enemies, we should find in each life sorrow and suffering enough to disarm any hostility.

Henry Wadsworth Longfellow

The greatest good you can do for another is not just share your riches, but to reveal to him his own.

Benjamin Disraeli

The best portion of a good man's life, his little nameless, unremembered acts of kindness and love.

William Wordsworth

Forget injuries, never forget kindness.

Confucius

Beginning today, treat everyone you meet as if they were going to be dead by midnight. Extend them all the care, kindness and understanding you can muster. Your life will never be the same again.

Og Mandino

No act of kindness, no matter how small, is ever wasted.

Aesop

The ideals which have lighted my way, and time after time have given me the courage to face life cheerfully have been Kindness, Beauty, and Truth. The trite subjects of human efforts, possessions, outward success, luxury...have always seemed to me contemptible.

Albert Einstein

22

THIS TIME TOMORROW
IT WILL STILL BE NOW

In one day of our life, we have 24 precious hours of living time. That adds up to 168 hours a week and 8,736 hours a year. If we live to the average life expectancy in the U.S. of 78 years, that grants us 681,408 hours of life, or 28,470 days. Without a doubt, our body is a pretty amazing battery to power our life adventure, the original "DieHard."

If we subtract eight hours of sleep from each day, that leaves us with 454,272 waking hours over the course of our lifetime. Now let's say we spend some of these waking hours not focused in the present moment.

If we do this 25 percent of the time then for every minute we are alive we spend 45 seconds focused in the present moment and 15 seconds drifting. This means if we lived to the age of 78, we would spend 109,824 total hours drifting, the equivalent of 4,576 days or 12 1/2 years of our life!

Now think of our life as being a boat out at sea. Using this same breakdown, this means for 45 seconds of every minute we could steer our boat where wanted to go. But this would always be followed by 15 seconds in which the steering would stop working, the engine would cut off, and the boat would drift.

Think how much longer it would take us to get to our destination if this was how our boat operated. If we ever began to see this as a repeating pattern, like something that happened every waking minute of every day, we would probably have to fire the captain.

Well, in a sense we are on a boat. The boat is our mind and we are its captain. The sea is the sea of life in which we are immersed.

The more we can steer our boat, the faster we will get to where we want to go.

Living in the future or the past though is like subjecting our boat to endless drift. And if we have the misfortune to get permanently stuck on something other than the present moment, like the partially submerged shoals of a painful memory, it can render our boat inoperable or even cause it to sink.

So when you think about it, being in the present moment really is of ultimate importance. It's what gives us control over our journey. In fact, the present moment is probably the most precious commodity we own because time is the only commodity we can't get more of. We can't go bankrupt with our time and start over. When it is spent, it is spent. There is no going back for seconds.

And if time is money, like so many business folks believe, then being absorbed elsewhere in our mind for 25 percent of the time is like throwing away 25 percent of every paycheck. That is a pretty heavy tax to pay for not staying mindful.

Thought of in a different context, the present moment is also like the kitchen where we cook up the delicious experiences of our life. Every time we leave the kitchen we are no longer in charge of what we are creating. The oven may get too hot and burn our creations beyond recognition, or it may be too cool and they will be undercooked.

Or the wrong ingredients may get added into the mix, sometimes even bitter-tasting ingredients like worry, guilt, regret and fear. How would we know if we are not present? When we leave the kitchen, we have lost control of the flavor of our life.

You can see how this can happen when you consider the plight of the Mullah, the satirical character from traditional Sufi parables who doubles as a vehicle for universal wisdom. In this parable from, *The Fragrance of Faith: The Enlightened Heart of Islam* by Jamal Rahman, the Mullah wrestles with the challenge of staying mindful.

"During lunch break at work, the Mullah was getting exasperated. Every time he opened his lunchbox, it was a cheese sandwich. Day after day, week after week, it was the same, a cheese sandwich.

"I am getting sick and tired of this lousy cheese sandwich," complained the Mullah repeatedly. His co-workers finally gave him some advice; "Mullah, you don't have to suffer through a cheese sandwich over and over again. Kindly tell your loving wife to make you something different. She would be happy to if you asked."

"But I'm not married," replied the Mullah. By now, puzzled and confused, his colleagues asked, "Then who makes your sandwiches?"

"Well, I do!" replied the Mullah."

As the Mullah discovered, when we stay in present moment awareness, so much more of life's variety becomes available to us. When we are not in the present moment, the walls come down around our mind and close us off from the world.

We lock ourselves into a small room with no windows and limited options. The real world is passing by on the outside, but we wouldn't know it because we can't see beyond the obstruction of our misplaced awareness.

All we can do is find things inside our little room to keep us occupied. Suddenly these unsatisfying bits and pieces become our life because what we put our attention on, we become.

The mind is so good at fragmenting and leading us away from the moment at hand that we actually forget that the present moment is all we really have. There is nothing else. Time itself is just a theoretical construct. Yesterday and tomorrow don't even exist. They are just imaginary playthings of a mind adrift.

Admittedly, sometimes getting lost in our thoughts can be fun. Like reminiscing about a wonderful old romance or thinking about the prospects of finding new love. But compared to memories of the past or fantasies about the future, there is no companionship like the present moment. Anything is possible when we hang with the eternal always. Every interaction is as real as it gets because we are there to experience it fully.

Being in the now also strengthens our relationships because we become better listeners. Thinking about the dirt under our fingernails or some other unrelated thing when someone is telling us something important to them happens more frequently than most would probably dare admit.

But when two people are not fully present in a conversation, it's like two old computers with low bandwidths trying to share files. Nothing of any size or substance will get across. Our relationships just become hazy, missed opportunities.

Buddhism teaches that the present moment contains the seeds of all things, including liberation from samsara, which is the wheel of suffering. Our suffering increases because what Buddhists call our "monkey minds" which jump from thought to thought like monkeys swinging from tree to tree.

As the Buddha says, "More than those who hate you, more than all your enemies, an undisciplined mind does greater harm. More than your mother, more than your father, more than all your family, a well-disciplined mind does greater good."

"Ordinary thoughts course through our mind like a deafening waterfall," writes Jon Kabat-Zinn. To regain harmony in our life, Kabat-Zinn advises us to step away from the mental torrent so we can "rest in stillness to stop doing and focus on just being." Reestablishing our base in the present moment like he suggests lowers blood pressure, reduces fatigue, relieves stress and strengthens our life force.

So where are you right now? Are you here? Or are you somewhere else? How much of each day are you absorbed in something other than the present moment? How much of your life have you been truly present and accounted for? If there was ever a time to make amends, now is the time. In fact, now is the only time we can make amends.

Today, focus on staying in the living present and see how much more value you will squeeze out of it. Life unfolds its astonishing beauty in the eternal now so seize every second you can. There are 86,400 seconds in a single day. That is a lot of potential moments for happiness. When you do, your thinking will be clearer, your senses will be more alive, your heart will be more engaged and your highest potential will be within reach. You will always be where you need to be, right when you need to be there because now's timing is impeccable. Best of all, you will never again have to worry about all the moments you may have lost because the present moment lasts forever.

VOICES

The reason we want to go on and on is because we live in an impoverished present.

Alan Watts

Situations come to pass, they never come to stay. And when we allow them to pass and disappear into the past like shadows, our vibrant spiritual selves remain, powerful in the present moment. That is the constant, the unchanging, in an ever changing world.

Gail Pursell Elliot

Rejoice in the things that are present; all else is beyond thee.

Michel de Montaigne

The secret of health for both mind and body is not to mourn for the past, worry about the future, or anticipate troubles, but to live in the present moment wisely and earnestly.

Buddha

Now's an idea whose time has come,
The time of now has just begun,
It never gets ahead and never falls behind,
Now's on schedule every time,
It never runs slow, never runs fast,
It's the present moment, the only one that lasts,
Now's a thing that's only hard to grasp,
When we spend time living in the future or the past,
It needs no instructions on when, where, or how,
Now's always best when now is lived right now.

Monk

You must live in the present, launch yourself on every wave, find your eternity in each moment.

Henry David Thoreau

Rest in the Space Between thoughts

Made in the USA
Middletown, DE
16 April 2016